Duncan MacGregor

The Shepherd of Israel

Or, Illustrations of the Inner Life

Duncan MacGregor

The Shepherd of Israel
Or, Illustrations of the Inner Life

ISBN/EAN: 9783337101091

Printed in Europe, USA, Canada, Australia, Japan

Cover: Foto ©Lupo / pixelio.de

More available books at **www.hansebooks.com**

THE SHEPHERD OF ISRAEL:

OR,

ILLUSTRATIONS OF THE INNER LIFE.

BY THE
REV. DUNCAN MACGREGOR, M.A.,
MINISTER OF ST. PETER'S, DUNDEE, SCOTLAND.

NEW YORK:
ROBERT CARTER AND BROTHERS,
530 BROADWAY.
1870.

TO THE

REV. ALEXANDER DUFF, D.D., LL.D.,

PROFESSOR OF EVANGELISTIC THEOLOGY, NEW COLLEGE, EDINBURGH.

Reverend and Dear Sir:

I INSCRIBE YOUR NAME ON THIS LITTLE BOOK AS AN EXPRESSION OF WARM PERSONAL REGARD, AND ADMIRATION OF THE DISTINGUISHED GIFTS AND GRACES BESTOWED UPON YOU BY THE GREAT HEAD OF THE CHURCH, AND CONSECRATED WITH SUCH SELF-SACRIFICING DEVOTION TO HIS CAUSE.

DUNCAN MACGREGOR.

CONTENTS.

I.—THE SHEPHERD OF ISRAEL.

PAGE

"Give ear, O Shepherd of Israel, thou that leadest Joseph like a flock; thou that dwellest between the cherubim, shine forth. Before Ephraim and Benjamin and Manasseh stir up thy strength, and come and save us," Psalm lxxx. 1, 2, . . . 9

II.—THE KING'S DAUGHTER.

"The king's daughter is all glorious within: her clothing is of wrought gold. She shall be brought unto the king in raiment of needlework: the virgins her companions that follow her shall be brought unto thee. With gladness and rejoicing shall they be brought: they shall enter into the king's palace," Psalm xlv. 13-15, ... 32

III.—THE CLOUD AND THE SUNSHINE.

"Although my house be not so with God; yet he hath made with me an everlasting covenant, ordered in all things, and sure: for this is all my salvation, and all my desire, although he make it not to grow," 2 Samuel xxiii. 5, ... 54

IV.—THE UNKNOWN WAY AND THE KNOWN GUIDE.

PAGE

"And I will bring the blind by a way that they knew not; I will lead them in paths that they have not known: I will make darkness light before them, and crooked things straight. These things will I do unto them, and not forsake them," Isaiah xlii. 16, ... 76

V.—REMEMBERING ALL THE WAY.

"And thou shalt remember all the way which the Lord thy God led thee these forty years in the wilderness, to humble thee, and to prove thee, to know what was in thine heart, whether thou wouldest keep his commandments or no. And he humbled thee, and suffered thee to hunger, and fed thee with manna. . . . Thy raiment waxed not old upon thee, neither did thy foot swell, these forty years. . . . As a man chasteneth his son, so the Lord thy God chasteneth thee, . . . to do thee good at thy latter end," Deut. viii. 2–5, 16, ... 99

VI.—THE STRANGER IN THE EARTH.

"I am a stranger in the earth," Psalm cxix. 19, . 129

VII.—THE FRIENDSHIP OF THE SAVIOUR AND THE SAVED.

"Henceforth I call you not servants; for the servant knoweth not what his lord doeth: but I have called you friends; for all things that I have heard of my Father I have made known unto you," John xv. 15, ... 152

CONTENTS.

VIII.—CLOSER THAN A BROTHER.

PAGE

"And there is a friend that sticketh closer than a brother," Proverbs xviii. 24, ... 171

IX.—THE FIERY TRIAL.

"Beloved, think it not strange concerning the fiery trial which is to try you, as though some strange thing happened unto you: but rejoice, inasmuch as ye are partakers of Christ's sufferings; that, when his glory shall be revealed, ye may be glad also with exceeding joy," 1 Peter iv. 12, 13, . . 180

X.—THE TRIUMPH.

"Beloved, think it not strange concerning the fiery trial which is to try you, as though some strange thing happened unto you: but rejoice, inasmuch as ye are partakers of Christ's sufferings; that, when his glory shall be revealed, ye may be glad also with exceeding joy," 1 Peter iv. 12, 13, . . 205

XI.—THE WONDERS OF THE BIBLE.

"Thy testimonies are wonderful," Psalm cxix. 129, . 223

XII.—TAKE HEED HOW YE HEAR.

"Take heed how ye hear," Luke viii. 18, . . . 238

XIII.—AS WHITE AS SNOW.

"Come now, and let us reason together, saith the Lord: though your sins be as scarlet, they shall be as white as snow; though they be red like crimson, they shall be as wool," Isaiah i. 18, ... 267

XIV.—THE GREAT MULTITUDE.

"After this I beheld, and, lo, a great multitude which no man could number, of all nations, and kindreds, and people, and tongues, stood before the throne, and before the Lamb, clothed with white robes, and palms in their hands; and cried with a loud voice, saying, Salvation to our God which sitteth upon the throne, and unto the Lamb. . . . These are they which came out of great tribulation, and have washed their robes, and made them white in the blood of the Lamb. . . . They shall hunger no more, neither thirst any more; neither shall the sun light on them, nor any heat. For the Lamb, which is in the midst of the throne, shall feed them, and shall lead them unto living fountains of waters; and God shall wipe away all tears from their eyes," Rev. vii. 9–17, . . . 280

XV.—TIMES OF REFRESHING.

"And when they had prayed, the place was shaken where they were assembled together; and they were all filled with the Holy Ghost, and they spake the word of God with boldness. And the multitude of them that believed were of one heart and of one soul: neither said any of them that aught of the things which he possessed was his own; but they had all things common. And with great power gave the apostles witness of the resurrection of the Lord Jesus: and great grace was upon them all," Acts iv. 31–33, ... 292

XVI.—HE THAT WINNETH SOULS IS WISE.

THE LIFE AND LABORS OF THE REV. WM. C. BURNS.

"He that winneth souls is wise," Proverbs xi. 30, . 316

I.

THE SHEPHERD OF ISRAEL.

Ps. lxxx. 1, 2.

"Give ear, O Shepherd of Israel, thou that leadest Joseph like a flock; thou that dwellest between the cherubim, shine forth. Before Ephraim and Benjamin and Manasseh stir up thy strength, and come and save us."

OUR object in sending forth this messenger is to speak a word for Christ to those whom we have no strength to reach by the living voice. Thou who guidest the stars in heaven, guide it where it will speak a word in season!

This psalm was written in a time of sore trouble. Some of its strains are as plaintive as the Lamentations of Jeremiah. (V. 4, 5, 6.) The Church is in tears. She dips her morsel in the vinegar. She feels herself under God's frown. She feels as if he were angry against the prayer of his people. And her enemies enjoy their cruel triumph. That mighty Arm, so often in days past revealed in the splendor of its power in her defence, is no longer made bare. Israel is an easy prey to their enemies. The Vine which God brought out of Egypt and planted in the promised land—the noble Vine of the Old Testament Church—the Vine which covered the hills of Canaan with its shadow, and whose boughs were like the goodly cedars—the Vine which in the days of David and Solomon overspread the land from the Mediterranean to the Euphrates, and from Lebanon to the wilderness of Beersheba—is plucked, wasted, devoured, burnt. It was in such a cloudy and dark day that the Church raised this cry to God. Like the disciples in the storm who awoke Jesus, saying, "Master, carest thou not that we perish?" she lifts her voice to him who is a very present help in trouble. It is told of Martin Luther that he always sang the forty-sixth psalm in his distresses, and called it the war-song of the Church. But it was the Church's war-song long before Luther. Thirty centuries ago she had learned to sing, "The Lord on high is mightier than the noise of many waters, yea, than the mighty waves of the sea:" "The Lord is my Rock and my fortress, and my deliverer; my God, my strength in whom I will trust: my buckler and the horn of my salvation, and my high tower."

Let us consider three points:

    I. God's *Name*—"The Shepherd of Israel, who leadeth Joseph like a flock."

    II. God's *Dwelling-place*—"Between the cherubim."

    III. The *Church's Prayer*—"Shine forth: stir up thy strength, and come and save us."

I. God's *Name*. The Shepherd of Israel is the name to which the distressed Church appeals. This name to her is an ointment poured forth, and illustrates better than any other the care, and love, and tenderness of God. "The Lord is my Shepherd, I shall not want." "He shall feed his flock like a Shepherd." In the

New Testament the name is applied specifically to Jesus. He applies it to himself, "I am the good Shepherd."

The words, "that leadest Joseph like a flock," describe the Shepherd's whole work in guiding Joseph from Egypt to Canaan. There is peculiar fulness and breadth in the word "leadest." There is a density, so to speak, in the language of inspired poetry which it is difficult to express in common words. We almost shrink from analyzing it logically, as we shrink from cutting a rose in two. These lovely branches of the Tree of Life, laden with twelve manner of fruits, and whose very leaves are for the healing of the nations, refuse to be compressed into our more or less artificial forms. Better to pluck the fruit off them as they grow in the garden of God! Better to eat the bread than to describe its chemical constituents! One loves to take a word like this as it stands, and drink salvation out of it. If we might venture to subdivide it, with the view of opening up its treasures, we should say that along with the main idea of *guiding*, it includes the kindred ones of *feeding* and *watching over*.

1. The Shepherd of Israel *guides* Joseph.

"Thou leddest thy people like a flock by the hand of Moses and Aaron." As the cloudy pillar went before Israel, and fixed their resting-places, and guided them all through the wilderness—a cooling shade by day and a shining lamp by night—so the Shepherd of Israel guides Joseph like a flock to the end. And Joseph follows the Shepherd of Israel. "These are they that follow the Lamb whithersoever he goeth." The desert is long and weary. You know not whither to go. You are apt to lose your way, and wander in by-paths, and once astray you cannot find your way back again.

But he knows the way thoroughly. He has led Joseph like a flock in all generations from Abel downwards. He knows the best way for *you*. "Thine ear shall hear a voice behind thee, saying,'This is the way, walk ye in it." (Isa. xxx. 21.) He knows how fast each sheep and lamb in his innumerable flock can be led.

Some have a short journey to heaven. They speed their way home. They pass the milestones quickly in the daylight. The Shepherd of Israel takes long steps with them, and they reach Canaan soon. A blessed gale blowing fresh from the heavens wafts these happy voyagers to the shores of glory. The whole range of Christian Biography abounds with examples. Let me name Brainerd and Martyn, James Halley and Robert M'Cheyne, Mackintosh and Hedley Vicars, Hewitson and David Sandeman. Others cannot be led so fast. They would die. The Shepherd of Israel knows this.

O blessed Shepherd: with what unerring wisdom he guides Joseph as he is able to bear it! And when Joseph backslides, he restores him—when Joseph falls, he lifts him up—when Joseph is weary and footsore, he bears him as on eagles' wings. "My presence shall go with thee, and I will give thee rest;" "I will bring the blind by a way that they know not." (Exod. xxxiii. 14; Isa. xlii. 16.) And he bears all the costs of the journey. "My grace is sufficient for thee, for my strength is made perfect in weakness." "I will never leave thee, nor forsake thee." Ah! that word, "Never leave thee," reaches through the darkest hours of temptation, the chillest seasons of desertion, the deepest waters of affliction, the hottest fires of persecution; it reaches unto death, through death and the grave to the eternal rest beyond.

It tests the shepherd's skill to lead his flock across a deep, dark, swelling river. The Shepherd of Israel leads every sheep and lamb of his innumerable flock safe across the Jordan of death. He carries them in his arms to the farther shore. He never lost one. As Israel walked through the Red Sea between two high crystal walls,—as Jordan's waters were driven back, and the white-robed priests stood in the middle of its channel bearing the golden ark until the last of Israel passed over,—so Jesus stands in the middle of the stream of death, until the last of his flock has entered the Promised Land. In the presence of the Shepherd of Israel, Death, which to the eye of sense is a spectre terror-crowned, becomes the messenger of peace to call Joseph home. "The sucking child shall put his hand upon the cockatrice's den." We saw a beautiful verification of these words some time ago. Next door to ours, on a communion Sabbath morning, a little man, just six years old, was taken home to glory. The day before he died, he said to his aunt, "Aunt, there's a great change in me;" and seeing her look sad, he said, "It's in my soul, I mean. I never felt Jesus so near. I feel as if I could touch him. Surely the angel will be coming soon now!" To dry her fast-falling tears the dear little saint added, "I should like to be with you a little longer, and do some work for Jesus; but the angel is coming very soon!"

> "Asleep in Jesus! blessed sleep!
> From which none ever wakes to weep;
> Asleep in Jesus! peaceful rest,
> Whose waking is supremely blest."

2. The Shepherd of Israel *feeds* Joseph.

He who said to Peter, "Feed my sheep," "Feed my lambs," is careful to feed them himself. He has provided a fold, and green pastures, and quiet waters, and under-shepherds to tend the sheep under his own eye. The fold is the Church of Christ. The green pastures are his word and ordinances. The still waters are the fulness of spiritual blessings treasured up in him. The under-shepherds are faithful pastors. Christ's pastures are always green. Throughout the whole range of God's blessed book he leads Joseph from spot to spot, feeding him with food convenient for him. He who fed millions with manna in the desert feeds millions now in the green pastures of the word. He knows what pasture best suits every sheep and lamb in his flock. As the wants of the flock are various, the pastures are various. He has strong meat for the strong, he has milk for babes. "He gathers the lambs with his arm, and carries them in his bosom." He leads Joseph from place to place. Sometimes he feeds you in luxuriant pastures, and anon he withdraws you to pick the grass amongst the rocks, to feed on the bitter herbs of reproof, and repentance, and godly sorrow. See the beautiful variety of gifts which, for this end, he dispenses to the under-shepherds who feed his flock. Paul and Apollos and Cephas are yours, if you are Christ's. One star differs from another star in glory. One, like the Baptist, comes preaching repentance, with voice like the strong wind that bloweth; and one, like Barnabas, is a son of consolation. One pierces with arrows of conviction; another pours in the oil of gladness. One has drunk largely of Christ's love, like John; and another, like Paul, is mighty in the deep things of God; and all to meet the varied wants of the sheep and lambs of Christ.

3. The Shepherd of Israel *watches over* Joseph.

In the wildernesses of the East, infested by wolves, and lions, and thieves, shepherds watch their flocks all night. In the wilderness of this world worse thieves, wolves, and lions prowl abroad. Hence the Shepherd of Israel is ever on the watch. From heaven—that high place of prospect and of power—he looks down with eyes of flame, and sees every danger and snare and enemy. (Ps. cxxi. 4; Luke xxii. 31, 32; Zech. ii. 5.) A great work has been intrusted to him. His Father's glory, and millions of precious souls—dear to God as the apple of his eye, dear to himself as the jewels of his crown—are put under his care. Thousands of his flock are in every corner of the wide world. He watches over them all. If he had not watched over the wise virgins when they slept, what had become of them? If he had not watched over Peter in the hour of his melancholy fall, what had become of him? "Fear not, little flock; it is your Father's good pleasure to give you the kingdom." No lion can harm you, no robber can spoil him of his treasures. As he never *has* lost one, so he never shall. Tenderly as a mother watches her sick child, and forgets sleep and rest for its sake,—and hangs over it from morning to night, and from night to morning—and guards its broken slumbers—and interprets its little cries and signals—and tries to hide her tears from its observation: so will the Shepherd of Israel watch over Joseph—over the very feeblest of his lambs and sheep, until they are safe in the fold above!

II. God's *Dwelling-place:* "Between the cherubim."

The mercy-seat stood between the cherubim, so that the words before us mean, "Thou that dwellest *upon the mercy-seat.*" The answer which the Old Testament gives to the question, Where is God? is, *Between the cherubim*—upon the mercy-seat. The answer which the New Testament gives to the same question is, "*God is in Christ*, reconciling the world unto himself, not imputing unto men their trespasses." (2 Cor. v. 19.) God is *on the mercy-seat* was the joyful news heard from the tabernacle courts. *God is in Christ* is the surpassingly more joyful news heard from the cross. These two mean precisely the same thing. It follows that the mercy-seat was a type of Christ—one of the most memorable types. The reasons are these: —the mercy-seat was a massive plate of gold, which, like a lid, covered the ark of the testimony. The great Puritans, and the school of Boston and the Erskines, saw in this plate of gold a symbol at once of the Godhead and the sinlessness of Jesus. The two Tables of the Law were in the ark; the mercy-seat covered them and hid them out of sight. The mercy-seat was as broad as the tables and broader: and thus, although the Law is exceeding broad, Christ's obedience and sufferings unto the death are commensurate with its highest requirements —they magnified it, and made it honorable. (Isa. xlii. 21; Rom. x. 4.) The law was honored when the golden mercy-seat covered it above, and the fragrant Shittim wood of the ark inclosed it around; but it was still more honored when Jesus said, "Lo, I come: in the volume of the book it is written of me, I delight to do thy will, O my God: yea, thy law is within my heart." (Ps. xl. 7, 8.) The law and its curse were hid in the ark. You could not have seen them. The law was covered while mercy was displayed. How was it covered? By the mercy-seat. That broad plate of massive gold came between and concealed the law and its thunder from your sight. Thus Christ comes between us and the Law's dreadful demands and unescapable terrors to-day. On the great day of Atonement, (Lev. xvi.) if you had entered in, with Aaron, through the veil, into the most holy place, you could not have seen the law nor read its sentence. You would have seen the mercy-seat sprinkled with atoning blood, the cloud of glory resting upon it, the cherubim overshadowing it, and the Shepherd of Israel dwelling between the cherubim, waiting to be gracious; while Aaron, amid a cloud of incense, presented the prayers of the people that thronged the temple courts; and from the golden mercy-seat you would have heard a voice issue, sweet as the music of paradise—a voice which was afterwards to ring round the world: "Come now, and let us reason together, saith the Lord: though your sins be as scarlet, they shall be as white as snow; though they be red like crimson, they shall be as wool." (Isa. i. 18; Exod. xxv. 22.)

So now God is in Christ. You see the law and its curse no more, for "there is now no condemnation to them that are in Christ Jesus." You see Christ crucified, and in him you see the law magnified and its curse taken away. God has set him forth to be a propitiation, through faith in his blood, and this propitiation, or propitiatory, is the mercy-seat of the King of kings. Before it stands our Advocate, with his golden censer, and amid fragrant incense which fills all heaven, he presents our prayer before his Father. (Heb. iv. 16; Rev. viii. 3.)

Come, then, to the Shepherd of Israel who dwells between the cherubim. No voice of doom was ever heard by suppliant there. But remember, there is no other meeting-place with God: "There I will meet with thee," and there only. Not on Sinai, for the God of Sinai is a consuming fire. Not in the outer courts of the temple, for it will profit you nothing to be in Jerusalem unless you see the King's face. Above all, not in "the great cathedral of immensity," as many of the great and learned in our time love to speak, for the universe, with all its wonders, can give no answer to the question, "How shall man be just with God?" There is no spot on earth where guilty man can meet God in peace, but the mercy-seat between the cherubim.

But there you are safe. There may you see the infinite love and loveliness of God. Not elsewhere. For guilt "makes cowards of us all." Like those dense fogs in London, which make the sun look fiery red, so the fear which guilt plants in the spirit represents God, simply as a God of wrath and terror. And there *is* one red letter in God's name—"He will by no means clear the guilty." In these circumstances, it is impossible for a sinner to see the ineffable beauty of his character. As Chalmers loved to express it, "For one who has never seen a beautiful landscape, it is impossible to admire it, if it has but suddenly started into visibility when illumined by the fires of a volcano. The spectator, in such a case, will feel more anxiety about his safety than admiration for the scenery around him. And thus, a man appalled by a sense of guilt, and by 'a certain fearful looking for of judgment and fiery indignation which shall devour the adversaries,' cannot admire the character of God." But, oh! look to the Shepherd of Israel as dwelling between the cheru-

him — see how mercy and truth there meet together, how righteousness and peace have kissed each other — see how all God's attributes are revealed over the mercy-seat like rainbow hues, and can you repress the prayer of Moses as he stood by the cleft of the rock, "I beseech thee, show me thy glory"?

Walking lately along Princes Street in Edinburgh, I instinctively turned my eye to look at yon grand and gray Castle rock. Seeing the grim guns planted round the battlements, the thought arose, "If these guns were fired, I should be in danger of being blown to atoms." I turned up the hill, crossed the drawbridge, entered the castle gate, and wheeling round to the left, mounted to the top of the tower. What did I see? That I was *behind the guns*, and that, although they should all open fire and bombard the metropolis, I was safe.

My brother! as long as you are out of Christ the Rock of Ages, God has planted his cannon against you. Flee to him—enter in by the wicket-gate, and you will find out the blessed truth, that "the Name of the Lord is a strong tower; the righteous runneth into it, and is safe."

III. The *Church's Prayer:* "Shine forth: stir up thy strength, and come and save us."

1. Shine forth in token of thy *gracious presence*. Thou seemest to be angry against the prayer of thy people—most justly mightest thou be angry. But as the dawn chases away the darkness, as the sun breaks forth after a dismal tempest, do thou shine forth, and bring to thy weeping Church a glorious day. Though thou wast angry with us, let thine anger be turned away. Let the Sun of Righteousness arise on us with healing in his wings. One smile of thy face, one glimpse of thy love, would turn our mourning to dancing, our sackcloth to garments of salvation, our sad complaints to gladsome praises. Although we have eaten the bread of tears—although we have dipped our morsel in the vinegar—although we have drunk of Marah's bitter waters—shine forth, and our sorrow shall be turned into joy. Shine forth as

at Bethel, when Jacob saw the dream-ladder, with the angels of God ascending and descending upon it, and waking, cried, "This is none other but the house of God, and this is the gate of heaven." Shine forth as at the completion of Solomon's temple, when "the cloud filled the house, and the priests could not stand to minister by reason of the cloud, for the glory of the Lord filled the house of God." As the fire descended upon Carmel and consumed Elijah's sacrifice, in token of thy gracious acceptance, let it now descend upon us, and let all the people cry, with the same awe-struck reverence as then, "The Lord he is the God, the Lord he is the God." Shine forth, and make even the dullest feel that *God is here*. What a new feeling it would be to many! When earthly royalty is present in an assembly, what an almost oppressive sense of awe—what hushed expectancy even before its arrival! But let the King of kings shine forth with his train of attendant angels—let the children of Zion be joyful in their King—let all the churches of the saints have "light and gladness and joy and honey"

—and let even the rebellious draw near to touch his golden sceptre! *

2. Stir up *thy strength*, and come to save us.

"Before Ephraim, Benjamin, and Manasseh." These three tribes marched immediately after the ark in the wilderness. So the meaning is, that God would make bare his arm in the sight of all the tribes of Israel. The Church pleads the former displays of God's power, and asks for a renewal of the same splendid interpositions of the Arm for which nothing is impossible. "Stir up thy strength"—win fresh victories over Satan, crown thyself with fresh spoils. (Ps. xlv. 3–5; Isa. li. 9, 10.) Our argument should be the same to-day. "Is anything too hard for the Lord?" "Why should it be thought a thing incredible with you that God should raise the dead?" The might and majesty of his arm

---

* In a church in G—— we once saw on the fly-leaf of an old Bible, after the name and date, these words, written in a beautiful hand: "*A day never to be forgotten.*" The date was seventy years old. "Ah!" thought we, "on that day the Shepherd of Israel shone forth from between the cherubim on the writer's soul!"

is the same as when he cut the sea in two—when he drove back Jordan's waters—when he made the dry bones in Ezekiel's valley stand up on their feet an exceeding great army. The Church often uses holy boldness. "Awake, awake, put on strength, O arm of the Lord." She speaks as if this arm were asleep. Sirs, our great want is the want of power. It is not so much better preaching, nor an exacter exegesis, nor a profounder theology, that we need. It is the manifestation of God's power. "Who hath believed our report, and to whom is the arm of the Lord revealed?" We need the power which the Son of God wielded when he gave sight to the blind, ears to the deaf, speech to the dumb, feet to the lame, cleansing to the leper, life to the sheeted dead; the power which the angel put into the healing waters of Bethesda; the power which armed the fisherman's words, as they struck across the street with such piercing force, that three thousand could not repress the cry, "Men and brethren, what shall we do?" We need the power which would solemnize the thoughtless in our congregations, and rouse those who are asleep in their sins. We need the power which would turn back the tide of Sabbath profanation which is steadily rising, and which would fill all classes of the community with reverence for the word of God. And when we look at the frequency with which the Spirit of glory and of God is promised—when we remember that Jesus' parting words to the eleven were, "Behold, I send the promise of my Father upon you, but tarry ye in the city of Jerusalem until ye be *endued with power* from on high"—when we see the frequent fulfilments of the promise along the whole line of the Church's history, and how the very breath of God played around a Luther, a Knox, a Wesley, a Chalmers, we ought to feel quite an infinite hopefulness in lifting up the prayer, "Stir up thy strength, and come and save us!" God of Pentecost, stretch forth thine hand—*use what instruments thou pleasest*—only let signs and wonders be done in the name of thy Holy Child Jesus! Reveal the power which planted the Christian faith at first by apostles and evangelists—which planted the

Reformed Faith in Scotland three centuries ago by Knox and Melville—which in our own times has made many a wilderness and solitary place be glad, and many a desert rejoice and blossom as the rose!

POST TENEBRAS LUCEM SPERO.

II.

THE KING'S DAUGHTER.

Ps. xlv. 13-15.

"The king's daughter is all glorious within : her clothing is of wrought gold. She shall be brought unto the king in raiment of needlework : the virgins her companions that follow her shall be brought unto thee. With gladness and rejoicing shall they be brought : they shall enter into the king's palace."

THERE is a striking resemblance between this psalm and the Song of Solomon. The general plan of the Song is outlined here by "the pen of the ready writer;" the filling in of the details was left to Solomon—just as God gave David the pattern of the temple, but employed Solomon to build it. The theme is the Church's espousals to Christ, and it is illustrated with a profusion of gorgeous imagery. Its magnitude is plain from the fact, that an entire book of the Bible is devoted to the unfolding of it, and that allusions to it, like threads of gold, run through the whole Bible. Consider:

I. The Bride's *new name*—"The King's daughter."

What a title, and what privileges it involves! She is the King's daughter for two reasons: 1. She is *born* of God; and 2. She is *espoused* to the Son of God. She is the King's daughter by birth as well as by marriage—by a heavenly origin as well as a heavenly bond. Her dignity rests both on blood relationship and on the dearest affinity.

Amazing fact! she was once an alien and an enemy. "Her father was an Amorite, and her mother an Hittite." She was once condemned to die. She was once a child of the devil, and bore his image, did his work, wore his livery. This is the state of all of us by nature. "The crown is fallen from our head." Have you ever thought, when Nebuchadnezzar was driven from his throne, and sent to herd with the beasts of the field, until "his hair grew like eagles' feathers, and his nails like birds' claws," with what sad surprise must the passers-by have looked over the hedge, and said, "That was a king once—once he filled the proudest of earthly thrones, and could make or unmake kings at his pleasure, though now sunk so low." With still sadder surprise must angels look down from heaven's golden battlements on man as he eats the husks of sin, and say, "That was a king once, though now so fallen!"

1. But the day of *regeneration* came, and she who was once an enemy is admitted into dearest friendship; she who was once condemned is pardoned, and not only pardoned, but exalted to sit with Christ in heavenly places. What dignity is this! Talk not of earthly coronets, of royal rank, of gentle blood. The proudest Bourbon or Plantagenet is by nature a child of wrath even as others; while this new birth makes the vilest sinner a child of God, a member of the royal family of heaven. "Behold what manner of love the Father hath bestowed upon us, that we should be called the sons of

God." And as a Father loves his children, admits them into his presence, supplies all their wants, sympathizes with their sorrows, and lovingly corrects their faults, so does God deal with his adopted sons and daughters. They enjoy " a Father's pity, a Father's love, a Father's open house, a Father's open heart."* The Bride of the Lamb, then, is the King's daughter on account of her new birth. There is royal blood in her veins.

2. And then came the day of her *espousals* to the Lord Jesus. Once she was married to the law, but that marriage is now dissolved. She is become dead to the law by the body of Christ. (Rom. vii. 4.) Her eyes are opened to see that he is fairer than the children of men; that naught else is to be compared to him; that naught else can satisfy the heart but he; that naught else is worthy of a thought but he. " Who would not part with farthings for guineas?" said Romaine. Her will is divinely bent to make choice of him, to renounce father and mother for him, to count all things loss for

* Candlish's "Fatherhood of God," p. 197.

him. Her heart is drawn to make a complete surrender of herself to him. "I love his *person* as God-man. His divinity is the almighty prop on which my clinging soul would lean, and on his human heart would I ever draw for sympathy. Here is the ladder whose foot rests on the earth, whose top leans against the jasper wall of heaven. I love his *offices* as Prophet, Priest, and King. I love his *marriage covenant*—it is ordered in all things and sure. I love his *fellowship*. Those meetings with him in the pavilion of prayer, those glimpses of him through the lattice, are the beginnings of heaven. I love his *cross;* there is a fragrance even about *it*, and for his sake, like Simon of Cyrene, I cheerfully bear it after him. I love his *crown*. Heaven is heaven to me, because he is there—the Lamb in the midst of the throne." "What things were gain to me, those I counted loss for Christ. Yea doubtless, and I count all things but loss for the excellency of the knowledge of Christ Jesus my Lord." (Phil. iii. 7, 8.)

Thus is the soul espoused to Christ. And thus, believer, you are one with him. You lose your individuality in him. You take his name. (Compare Jer. xxiii. 6 with xxxiii. 16.) You are crucified with him, buried with him, risen with him to newness of life. You sit together with him in heavenly places, and, like *a jewel hid in a double case*, your life is hid with Christ in God; and when he who is your life shall appear, you also shall appear with him in glory.

II. The Bride's *character* — "All glorious within."

There is a wide difference between "the golden and the gilded," between the golden jewel and the gilded trinket. Grace is different from what Fraser of Brea styles "gilded grace." A hypocrite may be all glorious without. There may be the gilding of a sound creed, a fair profession, a blameless life, and many a charitable deed, while Satan, in some guise or other, holds the throne of the heart. The inexperienced eye cannot distinguish the gold from its gilded counterfeit; but when the day of trial comes— "the Refiner's day"—the gilding falls off, and the hypocrite is unmasked. But the King's daughter is all glorious within; she has bought of Christ "gold tried in the fire, and she is rich." The difference between the saint and the hypocrite may be stated thus: The deeper you pierce below the surface with a hypocrite, the worse he becomes; the deeper you pierce below the surface with a saint, the better he becomes, until, when you reach the heart, you find Christ reigning upon the throne, you find that he is all glorious within.

It will be asked, When so much corruption, so many deadly roots of sin, remain in every child of God, how can he be said to be all glorious within? We here touch upon the dreadful mystery of indwelling sin; but we ask, in reply, Was Job, then, not a saint when he said, "I have heard of thee with the hearing of the ear, but now mine eye seeth thee: wherefore I abhor myself, and repent in dust and ashes"? Was David not a saint when he cried, "My loins are full of a loathsome disease, and there is no soundness in my flesh"? Was Paul not a saint when a sense of inveterate sinfulness wrung the groan from his heart, "O wretched man that I am, who shall deliver me from the body of this death?"*

The King's daughter is all glorious within for two reasons :

1. Because *Christ reigns on the throne of her heart.* That heart which was once " the habitation of devils, and a cage of every unclean and hateful bird," has surrendered to him. In a day of power, his voice is heard, " Lift up your heads, ye gates; and be ye lifted up, ye everlasting doors, and the King of glory shall come in." Every bar is forced, the door swings upon its hinges, the King of glory enters, and possesses the throne.

In Sutherlandshire there lived, in the last age, one of those holy ministers whose names still survive as a fragrant reminiscence. He catechised the families of his flock every year. Catechising one day at a farm-house, when the

---

* The Puritans threw some light upon this point by the statement in Lev. xiii. 12, 13—" If the leprosy cover the whole body from head to foot, the priest shall pronounce the leper clean "—the reason being, that the seat of life was sound and strong, and able to throw off the disease. So if the war with sin is in the *members*, this is an evidence that its dominion in the heart is broken.

busy household were assembled, he asked the master of the house whether all were present. "All," said the other, "except the little girl who tends the cattle." "Call her," said the minister. The master hesitated, but the minister would not proceed until she came. Every one was catechised in turn. The little girl was asked, "Have you a soul?" "No," said she, with a slow, serious voice. "Have you never had a soul?" said the minister, nothing puzzled by the seemingly unfortunate answer. "Yes," she replied. "What became of it?" "One day lately," said she, "when keeping the cattle, I felt my soul very ill. 'The sorrows of death compassed me, and the pains of hell gat hold upon me.' I did not know what to do. I prayed and wept, but my soul was no better. At last I resolved to give it away to Jesus. I gave it to him. He took it, and he has it still. That's what I mean by saying that I have not a soul."

2. Because *she is a temple of the Holy Ghost*. As the cloud rested on the holy of holies, the Spirit dwells in the living temple. He

abides with the believer forever. "The blessed Spirit," says Matthew Henry, "useth not to change his lodging;" and wherever he dwells, he will not cease his work until the soul is changed into Christ's image from glory to glory. Ah, this makes the King's daughter all glorious within! No doubt iniquities prevail against her; the conflict between grace and sin is long and sore. "I am like the caterpillar," (we quote the touching words of the late Dr. Coldstream,) "which, having cast its old skin, abhors it, but is yet too feeble to creep away from it; it must wait till God shall give the necessary strength." The spark of grace often seems lost in a sea of corruption, but the indwelling of the Spirit is a guarantee that grace in the end will overcome; that the house of David will grow stronger and stronger, and the house of Saul weaker and weaker. In the hour of death the top-stone is put upon the work of sanctification. The soul receives its last baptism in the Holy Spirit's fire, and then, without spot or wrinkle, it joins the spirits of the just made perfect.

III. The Bride's *raiment*—"Wrought gold—needlework."

The richest material embroidered with the most exquisite skill. It is a robe which angels might envy, exceeding white as snow—a robe in which the wearer can stand unchallenged before the throne—a robe which will shine like the sun forever.

What *is* this clothing of wrought gold—this raiment of needlework? The *righteousness of Christ;* in other words, his perfect obedience and his atoning death.

1. His *perfect obedience*. He was made under the law. The law was in his heart. He rendered it divine obedience. He satisfied it in all the exceeding breadth and spirituality of its demands. At every step from the manger to the cross—every day of those incomparable thirty-three years—he "magnified it and made it honorable." And when you remember that he who rendered this perfect and plenary obedience was the King eternal, immortal, and invisible, you will see how his obedience shed a new lustre upon the law in the eyes of all

worlds, so that it was more honored by the obedience of Christ alone, than it had been dishonored by all the sins ever committed; or . (in the words of a great writer) that, "in virtue of Christ's obedience, it was inshrined in more august and inviolable sacredness than if Adam had never fallen." Divine obedience is far higher than angelic. This is the obedience by which the Royal Bride is made righteous. This is the robe of needlework in which she will enter the King's palace. It cost her elder Brother thirty-three years of spotless obedience to embroider it.

2. His *atoning death*. This is the complement of his perfect obedience. It was necessary not only to magnify the law by obedience, but to make reconciliation for the sins of the people. "The Lord laid upon him the iniquity of us all." The deep arrears must be paid. "He was wounded for our transgressions, he was bruised for our iniquities: the chastisement of our peace was upon him, and with his stripes we are healed." He "finished transgression, made an end of sin, made reconciliation for

iniquity, and brought in everlasting righteousness." "It is finished." Oh, blessed death, that procured for us everlasting life! Blessed satisfaction, that left us nothing to do but accept, with tears of joy, the unspeakable gift of God! Blessed cross, that purchased for us crowns of glory! Blessed sorrow, that brought us songs of joy! Blessed grave, in which our sins are buried forever!

But this righteousness must be imputed to us. We must be clothed with it. We must be wrapped in it from head to foot. In a "Directory for the Visitation of the Sick," by Anselm, Archbishop of Canterbury, in the eleventh century, the following remarkable words occur (Owen on Justification, Clark's ed., p. 17): "Dost thou believe that thou canst not be saved but by the death of Christ? The sick man answers 'Yes.' Then let it be said to him, 'Go to then, and whilst thy soul abideth in thee, put all thy confidence in this death alone, place thy trust in no other thing; commit thyself wholly to this death: cover thyself wholly with this alone; cast thyself wholly on this death; wrap thyself wholly in this death.' And if God would judge thee, say, 'Lord, I place the death of our Lord Jesus Christ between me and thy judgment, and otherwise I will not contend or enter into judgment with thee.' And if he shall say unto thee that thou art a sinner, say, 'I place the death of our Lord Jesus Christ between me and my sins.' And if he shall say to thee that thou hast deserved damnation, say, 'Lord, I put the death of our Lord Jesus Christ between thee and all my sins, and I offer his merits for my own, which I should have, and have not.' And if he shall say that he is angry with thee, say, 'Lord, I place the death of our Lord Jesus Christ between me and thy anger.'" *These men* understood the subject of imputed righteousness.

"Christ's blood and righteousness
Shall be the marriage dress,
In which I'll stand
At God's right hand,
Forgiven,
And enter rest
Among the blest
In heaven." *

* German hymn.

IV. The Bride's *companions*—"Virgins that follow her."

These are members of the Church, but the figure of a bridal train is employed to sustain the allegory. What a bright train the Royal Bride will have as she goes forth to meet the Bridegroom! Kings' daughters will be there, for every crowned head on earth shall one day bow at the foot of the cross. The daughter of Tyre shall be there—Tyre, the ancient emporium of the nations—to show that the merchandise of the world shall be holiness to the Lord. The kings of Sheba and Seba shall offer gifts. Jews and Gentiles will be there—representatives from all peoples, and tongues, and nations. "There are threescore queens, and fourscore concubines, and virgins without number." From the most unlikely places they come,*—from the snows of Lapland, and the sunny skies of

---

* A friend of ours, lately sojourning at Nice, met two Christian ladies from Russia. The name of M'Cheyne was mentioned. "Oh, tell your friends at home," said they, "how highly M'Cheyne's writings are prized, and how tenderly his name is cherished, by God's people, in Russia!"

Italy—from the four Continents of the world, they join the shining train, as it sweeps past to the King's palace—a multitude more and brighter than the stars in the Milky Way. Will *you* not join it? When so many will be saved, will you not be among the many?

They are *virgins*. They keep themselves unspotted from the world. They are weaned from its idols; they dread its contaminations. Their first care is to preserve the whiteness of their souls by daily washing in the blood of the Lamb. Their lamps are trimmed; their vessels are filled with oil. "Thou hast a few names even in Sardis which have not defiled their garments; and they shall walk with me in white: for they are worthy." (Rev. iii. 4.)

They *follow* the Royal Bride. They keep by her side in storm and sunshine. They follow her in the regeneration. They follow her in the search after her Beloved. (Song iii. 2, 3.) They follow her to the green pastures and the still waters. They follow her without the camp, bearing his reproach. Like Ruth, they leave father and mother to follow her. (Ruth

i. 16.) Like Caleb, they follow the Lord fully. When a crisis comes, and the question, "Who is on the Lord's side?" involves heavy issues, and hollow-hearted professors fly away like swallows before the storm, they follow her. When persecution comes, and Christ's faithful witnesses have to prophesy clothed in sackcloth, and perhaps to pass through a baptism of blood to the crown, they follow her: like Peden, when—the bloodhounds of persecution in full chase after him, and the lone moor his home—he thought of Richard Cameron gone to glory, and sighed, "Oh, to be with Richie!"

V. The Bride's *home-going*.

"She shall be brought unto the king in raiment of needlework . . . with gladness and rejoicing shall they be brought: they shall enter into the king's palace."

Now she is busy, like a betrothed one, preparing for the bridal-day—sometimes bright with hope, but oftener mourning her unreadiness to meet her Lord. She looks for him. She forgets her people and her father's house for him. She corresponds with him. She cries, "Until the day break and the shadows flee away, turn, my beloved: and be thou like a roe, or a young hart upon the mountains of Bether." Now the voyage is rough and the tempest is high, and, with "neither sun nor stars in many days appearing," sometimes "all hope of being saved is taken away:" at last the shores of Emmanuel's Land appear—angels stand beckoning—and the Royal Bride enters into the haven.

She shall see the King in his beauty. There will be a personal meeting. Here the marriage, like all royal marriages, is arranged by ambassadors. Joseph only speaks by an interpreter, and sometimes speaks roughly. She cannot see Jesus face to face now. But at last he will come out of the ivory palaces, and she shall be caught up to meet him in the clouds. These eyes shall see him—these arms shall embrace him—these ears shall hear the music of his voice. Oh, it was sweet to hear him say, "Come unto me, all ye that labor and are heavy laden, and I will give you rest;" but sweeter will it be to hear the joyful welcome from the throne, "Come, ye blessed!"

There will be an open declaration of his love to her before all worlds. Christ's love is very communicative. (Ps. xxv. 14.) As it is on earth, the parties are mutually pledged before the marriage, but no one knows it except the family and a few friends; when the marriage comes, it is published to the world. Thus souls are espoused to Jesus now by the ministry of the gospel, but few know it—sometimes they hardly know it themselves, by reason of dark clouds and shadows. But then the King will say from his throne, "These are my jewels—this is my Bride! For her I lay in the manger—for her I hung upon the cross—for her I lay in the grave. In a day of power, I espoused her to myself; I drew her with cords of love!"

"With gladness and rejoicing shall they be brought." Where are her tears and sorrows now? Where are her rags and deformities now? Where are the black spots she daily mourned over now? Where are her cares and crosses now? Where is the shame she bore for the name of Jesus now? "They shall enter into the King's palace." No sin yonder! No weeping, no harp on the willows yonder! No tempter yonder! No partings yonder! "And so shall we ever be with the Lord."

"Now while they were drawing towards the gate, behold a company of the heavenly host came out to meet them; to whom it was said by the two shining ones, These are the men that have loved our Lord when they were in the world, and that have forsaken all for his holy name; and he hath sent us to fetch them, and we have brought them thus far on their desired journey, that they may go in and look their Redeemer in the face with joy. Then the heavenly host gave a great shout, saying, 'Blessed are they that are called to the marriage-supper of the Lamb." (Rev. xix. 9.) There came out also at this time to meet them several of the King's trumpeters, clothed in white and shining raiment, who, with melodious voices, made even the heavens to echo with their sound. These trumpeters saluted Christian and his fellow with ten thousand welcomes from the world, and this they did with shouting and sound of trumpet. . . . Thus they came up to the gate. Now when they were come up to the gate, there was written over it in letters of gold, 'Blessed are they that do his commandments, that they may have right to the tree of life, and may enter in through the gates into the city.'

"Now I saw in my dream that these two men went in at the gate; and lo, as they entered, they were transfigured, and they had raiment put on that shone like gold. There were also some that met them with harps and crowns, and gave them the harps to praise withal, and the crowns in token of honor. Then all the bells in the city rang again for joy, and it was said unto them, 'Enter ye into the joy of the Lord.' I also heard the men themselves sing with a loud voice, saying, 'Blessing, honor, glory, and power be to him that sitteth upon the throne, and unto the Lamb for ever and ever!'

"Now, just as the gates were opened to let in the men, I looked in after them, and behold the city shone like the sun: the streets also were paved with gold, and in them walked many men with crowns on their heads, and palms in their hands, and golden harps to sing praises withal. There were also those that had wings, and they answered one another without intermission, saying, 'Holy, holy, holy is the Lord.' And after that they shut up the gates: which, when I had seen, I wished myself among them!"

"Angel voices sweetly singing,
Echoes through the blue dome ringing,
News of wondrous gladness bringing,
Ah! 'tis heaven at last!

"Sin forever left behind us,
Earthly visions cease to blind us,
Fleshly fetters cease to bind us,
Ah! 'tis heaven at last!

"On the jasper threshold standing,
Like a pilgrim safely landing,
See the strange, bright scene expanding—
Ah! 'tis heaven at last!

"Christ himself, the living splendor,
Christ the sunlight, mild and tender,
Praises to the Lamb we render—
Ah! 'tis heaven at last!"

FUIMUS—ERIMUS. (*The Jews' Motto.*)

III.

THE CLOUD AND THE SUNSHINE.

2 Sam. xxiii. 5.

"Although my house be not so with God; yet he hath made with me an everlasting covenant, ordered in all things, and sure: for this is all my salvation, and all my desire, although he make it not to grow."

THESE were the last words of David—the words he uttered before his spirit took its flight to join the general assembly of the redeemed. The words of the dying are heard with breathless attention. We listen reverently to the voice we shall soon hear no more. And they are long remembered. To this day we remember Jacob's dying words as he calmly gathered up his feet into the bed, "I have waited for thy salvation, O Lord." We remember Moses' grand farewell words ere he went up to the top of Pisgah to die, "Happy art thou, O Israel; who is like unto thee, O people, saved by the Lord!" We remember the heavenly smile that played on old Simeon's face as he took the Babe in his arms and said, "Lord, now lettest thou thy servant depart in peace, according to thy word: for mine eyes have seen thy salvation." And who can forget Paul's dying testimony? In his cold cell at Rome, with the four walls of a dungeon around him, and a bloody death before him, his eye kindled with the light of heaven as he wrote, "I am now ready to be offered, and the time of my departure is at hand. I have fought a good fight, I have finished my course, I have kept the faith. Henceforth there is laid up for me a crown of righteousness, which the Lord, the righteous judge, shall give me at that day: and not to me only, but unto all them also that love his appearing."

Our subject is the dying testimony of David. Let us deeply ponder the words spoken on that calm, bright death-bed. We have here:

I. The *cloud upon David's house*—"Although my house be not so with God."

II. The *sunshine in God's covenant*—"Yet he hath made with me an everlasting covenant," etc.

I. The *cloud upon David's house.*

Every saint has a cloud of some kind hanging over his house. God's dealings with his children resemble the coat of many colors which Jacob gave Joseph as a proof of his peculiar love. Crosses and comforts, trials and triumphs, dark dispensations and bright, are interwoven with divine grace and skill into a many-colored web. David was no exception. What a splendid career he ran, and yet how checkered! A shepherd-boy in Bethlehem, he is anointed by Samuel as Israel's future king; he slays Goliath and achieves a deathless name; he becomes the king's son-in-law; he is on the steps of the throne. Then Saul's jealousy pursues him; he is hunted as a partridge upon the mountains; for seven years he is a poor, homeless wanderer, with but a step between him and death. He ascends the throne, and the Philistines, Moabites, Edomites, harass him by turns; the sons of Zeruiah plot against him; his life is one continual storm of battle,—then comes his sad fall, followed quickly by the awful outbreaks in his family and the revolt of Absalom. And as his sun sets among dark clouds, he says with a heavy sigh, "My house is not so with God." Not as I wished it to be. Not as I fondly hoped it to be. Not as I often prayed it might be.

Three elements conspired to make the cloud upon David's house very dark.

1. The *state of his family*. The man after God's own heart had trained his children in the fear of God. We have his charge to Solomon on record, "And thou, Solomon my son, know thou the God of thy father, and serve him with a perfect heart and with a willing mind." (1 Chron. xxviii. 9.) The wise king tells how carefully his father had trained him, "I was my father's son, tender and only beloved in the sight of my mother. He taught me also, and said unto me, Let thine heart retain my words: keep my commandments, and live." (Prov. iv.

3, 4.) And no doubt he took equal pains with the rest. The sweet Psalmist of Israel would teach his sons to sing the praises of God. His palace would resound to the strains of that cunning harp whose melody breathed of heaven. He who felt a day in God's courts to be better than a thousand would bring his sons thither. He would bring them to the altar of God, unto God his exceeding joy. He would show them the white-robed priests offering the lambs of daily sacrifice morning and evening. He would bring them to the solemn feasts when the thousands of Israel were assembled. They saw the blood of the passover-lamb sprinkled on the door of his palace. Besides, God had promised to make him an house. "Thou hast spoken of thy servant's house for a great while to come." (2 Sam. vii. 19.) So that David's heart was set on the prosperity of his house. He hoped to see his sons rising up a godly and a princely race. Who can describe his disappointment? He saw them casting off the fear of God; giving loose reins to their lusts; his first-born Amnon committing deeds which it is impossible to read without the blush of infinite shame, and then murdered by his brother; Absalom a murderer, an adulterer, a traitor, hurried into eternity in the midst of his sins, leaving his father to cry with bleeding, anguished heart, "O my son Absalom! my son, my son Absalom! would God I had died for thee, O Absalom, my son, my son!" And—his house turned into a chamber of horrors, its glory almost utterly tarnished—he was now dying. No wonder that he cried bitterly, "Although my house be not so with God."

To a godly parent there is no such heartbreak as a godless child. The cruelty of Simeon and Levi planted a thorn in Jacob's dying pillow. "A foolish son is a grief to his father, and bitterness to her that bare him." Christian parents! let us train up our children for God, let us *daily pray for their conversion by name*, lest their sins be a cloud upon our homes.

2. The *state of the Church*. One of David's great aims was to build a temple to the Lord—to have the Ark inshrined in a palace of gold and cedar. His soul was on fire with the

thought, and he was willing to make any sacrifices for it. He could live in a tent himself—often in time of war had he slept on the tented field, the sod his couch and a stone his pillow; but he could not rest in a house of cedar while the Ark of God dwelt between curtains. He wished to make this the work of his life. He prayed for light, and God gave him the pattern of the house in writing, and made him understand it. The Spirit of God showed him the courts and holy places, the altar of burnt-offering and the altar of incense, and all the elaborate details of that glorious shrine. And amid wars and troubles he prepared abundantly before his death. He gave three thousand talents of gold and seven thousand talents of silver out of the royal treasury. He stirred up the people; and like fire in a prairie his holy zeal spread through the whole congregation of Israel, so that they gave five thousand talents of gold and ten thousand talents of silver. He never ceased making preparations as long as he lived. And yet he who planted the stars in heaven—some to blaze in the zenith and some to twinkle on the verge of the horizon, had ordained that Solomon and not David should build the temple. David received the pattern, provided the materials, stirred up the people, and had all things in readiness; Solomon built the house. "Whereas it was in thine heart to build an house unto my name, thou didst well that it was in thine heart: nevertheless thou shalt not build the house; but thy son shall build the house unto my name." (1 Kings viii. 18, 19.)

No doubt David bowed to God's gracious ordination; and yet did not a shade of disappointment cross his spirit? Did he not feel like Moses on the top of Pisgah when God told him that he could not enter into the land on which he gazed so wistfully? "Is my hope, then, to be blasted: is the object so long dearest to my heart not to be realized; and must I go down to the grave without seeing the Ark inshrined in a glorious temple in Jerusalem? The great desire of my life was to build an house to the Lord. I could be a houseless wanderer myself; but I dearly wished to 'find a place for the

Lord, an habitation for the Mighty God of Jacob.' Often have I prayed for this, and all seemed ready. But I must die without seeing my deepest wish fulfilled. 'My house is not so with God.'"

Now this is often the experience of a child of God. A young disciple is on fire to build a temple to the Lord. It is the one desire of his life. He prepares abundantly for it. He devotes himself perhaps to the ministry, and gives no sleep to his eyes and no slumber to his eyelids. And when he is ready to begin to build, God accepts the will for the deed, and calls him away to his blessed rest in the Lord. "Thou shalt not build me an house." Many bright examples could be cited from the annals of Christian biography. Ah! it costs a sore struggle meekly to learn that—

> "His state
> Is kingly; thousands at his bidding speed,
> And post o'er land and ocean without rest;
> *They also serve who only stand and wait.*"

Need I tell how Melanchthon hoped to build a temple, and labored with heart aglow to raise living stones from amid the dust and rubbish of a fallen world, and found, after years of comparatively fruitless toil, that "Old Adam was too hard for young Melanchthon." And the same experience occurs in another form. There is a floodtime of the Spirit. The river of God, which is full of water, pours its fertilizing inundation over the land. You hope that the temple is to be immediately built, that the kingdom of God is immediately to appear. There is a shaking among the dry bones—every church is a Bochim —there is a solemnity in the very streets—the tranquil things of eternity are brought very near; even secular journals take notice of it. There are cases of awakening in your own Sabbath class. You hope to see the temple built, and to take some little part in building it. But, alas, here and there the tide recedes—the world and the devil regain their old ascendency—many who promised well return like "the dog to his vomit, and like the sow that was washed to her wallowing in the mire;" and you say, in bitter disappointment, "My house is not so with God."

3. The *death-struggle with sin*. David had

sore combats with sin. The old man in him was strong, and often caused worse than mortal anguish. "My loins are filled with a loathsome disease." (Ps. xxxviii. 7.) Satan had smitten him down to the ground (Ps. cxliii. 3), and his great fall clouded his spirit to the end. Several of the Psalms (such as vi., xxxviii., cxlii., cxliii.) may be called first editions—Hebrew editions—of the seventh chapter of Romans. The struggle between the flesh and the spirit, between the Adam and the Christ in David's soul, explain those bursts of sorrow which alternate in the Psalms with tones of ecstatic bliss. This incessant life-long war made him moan on his death-bed, "My house is not so with God." There is no anguish like it. The loss of worldly goods, the sharpness of a first bereavement, all the sorrows you can name, are not to be compared with the agony of feeling sin's poison rankling within you, and the old serpent casting his nether folds around your soul, when you would fain be pure as Christ is pure.

And yet this qualified David to give expression to every form of spiritual feeling. In whatever state you be, he has been there before you. His trials were but the tuning of the instrument which the Spirit employed to express the various melodies which he designed for the consolation and edification of the Church in all ages. Hence the Psalms must ever be the best manual of devotion: all the thousand emotions of the believing heart are there. It is for the same reason that the seventh chapter of Romans is so precious to the saint struggling with indwelling sin. Paul reveals there the inner workings of his spirit. What should we do without that chapter? And let me add, that such a record as we have in Bunyan's "Grace Abounding" is fitted to be eminently helpful. Let me quote a single sentence. Speaking of Satan's temptations, he says, p. 65, "These things did sink me into very deep despair, for I concluded that such things could not possibly be found among them that love God. I often, when these temptations came upon me, did compare myself to the case of a child whom some gypsy hath by force taken up in her arms, and is carrying from friend and country. Kick sometimes I did, and also shriek and cry; but yet I was bound in the wings of temptation, and the wind would carry me away."

II. The *sunshine in God's covenant*. "Yet he hath made with me an everlasting covenant."

It has been quaintly but beautifully said, "There is an *Although* in this verse. The Christian has always an Although—some drawback, some thorn in his flesh, some crook in his lot, some bitter drop in his cup, some cloud on his sky. 'My house is not so with God,' my hope is not so bright, my work is not so prosperous as I expected. But there is a *Yet* here—'Yet he hath made with me an everlasting covenant;' and this Yet is enough to counterbalance and at last extinguish ten thousand Althoughs. Make an inventory of your trials and crosses—add them all together: this Yet is sufficient to turn your groans into songs, your night of weeping into a morning of joy!"

Let us turn our eyes to the sunshine of the covenant. "He hath made an everlasting covenant *with me*." The covenant of grace made with Christ before the foundation of the world is offered for our acceptance in the gospel. When we receive Christ and become one with him by a living faith, we become parties to the covenant. It is, as it were, presented for our signature; when we sign it, we are warranted to say, "He hath made an everlasting covenant *with me.*" Its provisions become ours.

This covenant is the charter of our inheritance—the title deeds of our estate. It secures for us all spiritual blessings in heavenly places in Christ. It does not give us present possession. For we walk by faith, not by sight; we are saved by hope. "The heir, as long as he is a child, differeth nothing from a servant, though he be lord of all; but is under tutors and governors until the time appointed of the father." Even the titles of his estate are in other and safer custody. He has to wait. And although he receives his maintenance from the estate, he is often in straits. Even so are we. "Our house is not so with God." But he has made an everlasting covenant with us. This covenant includes all the treasures of grace and glory. But these are not ours in possession—they are laid up for us in heaven. They are the objects of faith and hope. And when faith and hope are in lively exercise, this covenant is sufficient to sweeten every cross, to extract every sting, to lighten every burden, to irradiate every darkness. For:

1. It is *everlasting*. "I have loved thee with an everlasting love. (Jer. xxxi. 3.) The parties to it never die; the Mediator of it is the same yesterday, and to-day, and forever; its conditions cannot be changed, for they were confirmed and sealed forever in the blood of the Mediator; its promises can never fail, and its provisions can never be exhausted. What are these provisions? Not houses and lands, not corn and wine, not places and titles; but "all spiritual blessings in heavenly places in Christ." *God* is in this covenant—"I will be their God." *Christ* is in it—"This is my beloved Son: hear ye him." The *Holy Ghost* is in it—"He shall give you another Comforter, that he may abide with you forever." *Pardon* is in it—"Though your sins be as scarlet, they shall be as white

as snow." *Adoption* is in it—"Behold, what manner of love the Father hath bestowed upon us, that we should be called the sons of God!" *Sanctification* is in it—"Sin shall not have dominion over you, for ye are not under the law, but under grace." *Heaven* itself, with its beatitudes and its glories, is in it—"Eye hath not seen, nor ear heard, neither have entered into the heart of man the things which God hath prepared for them that love him." It is an *everlasting covenant*. How all earthly things pass away! The triumphal arch graces the triumph of a day and then withers. "We seize the flower, its bloom is fled." Every earthly pleasure will pall, every earthly fountain will be dried up, every earthly glory "will vanish like a bright exhalation in the evening." Dear young reader! *don't make your garlands of withered flowers*. Choose something that will last.

2. It is *ordered in all things*. (1.) In its *plan*: for it is the masterpiece of the manifold wisdom of God. (Rom. xi. 33.) (2.) In its *confirmation* by the testator's death; for this death turned the covenant into a testament, and made its pro-

mises payable to the heirs. That prince of evangelists, Robert Flockhart, who preached the gospel for forty years in the streets of Edinburgh, used to tell that, when he was in the army, on the morning of a battle, his comrade, who had to go into action, said before marching, "Robert, if I am killed, my desk, Bible, papers, and the rest of my property will be yours;" but "he came back alive," said Robert, "and I never got possession of the property!" But by the death of Christ the blessings of the covenant are free to the chief of sinners. *Come and welcome!* (3.) This covenant is ordered in respect of the *application* of its benefits to all who believe. For the Three Persons of the Godhead are the trustees, and they will see to it that the redemption purchased by Christ shall be infallibly applied to his people. (4.) And it is ordered in respect of the *Divine adaptation* of its provisions to the wants of believers. As the key fits into the wards of the lock, so do its provisions fit into the intricacies of your case, its light into the depths of your darkness, its love into the depths of your distress. It provides a balm for every wound, a cordial for every sorrow, a pardon for every sin.

3. It is *sure*. Confirmed by two immutable things in which it is impossible for God to lie—his word and his oath—and sealed by the two royal seals of Baptism and the Lord's Supper. Its blessings are called " the *sure mercies* of David." As surely as you take hold of it, will you one day walk the golden streets. God's word will never fail you. Clasp Christ's faithful hand now, and he will sustain you when flesh and heart fail. When Durham was on his death-bed, a cloud passed over his spirit, and he said to Principal Carstairs, "Think you I may venture my soul on the word, 'Him that cometh to me I will in no wise cast out'?" "If you had a hundred souls," said the other, "you might venture them all on that word."

It is " all the salvation and all the desire " of the dying saint. Look at David. Standing on the threshold of glory, the sunshine of the covenant not only brightens the dark valley, and reveals an open heaven and a radiant diadem, but it casts an illumination back on all the dark chapters of his history. Those sharp tribulations, whose meanings at the time were hid, are all intelligible now when the light of heaven is streaming in his face. Did he mourn over the state of his family? The covenant reveals that he is to be the head of the heathen, and that the coming Messiah will be his Son according to the flesh as well as his Lord. Did he mourn because God decreed that he should not build the temple? He sees that Solomon his son will build it, and that a greater Solomon will build a more glorious temple on Mount Zion, a temple of which the whole company of the redeemed shall be the living stones. Did he mourn over his inveterate sinfulness? The covenant reveals that Christ is his sanctification, that all his well-springs are in him, that at his glorious appearing he shall be satisfied with his likeness. "This is all my salvation and all my desire."

And it is so always. The covenant of grace is the solace of every dying saint. "The feeble among them at that day shall be as David." If you were to ask him, "*Have you had a heavy cross to bear?*" "Yes," he would say, "but Jesus bore the heavy end of it. It never galled my shoulder. When I was weary, he carried both myself and my cross. And I learned to look at the *bright* side of it."

"*Have you had fiery trials?*" "Yes, but the way of trial is the way to glory."

"Trials make the promise sweet,
Trials give new life to prayer:
Trials bring me to his feet,
Lay me low and keep me there."

"*Did God bring a winter on the work of sanctification in your soul?*" "Yes," he would reply, "many winters. I prayed for growth in grace, and he answered me by terrible things. I was often like a living man tied to a corpse. When I engaged in any spiritual duty, I was like an invalid climbing the pyramids. But I got sweet comfort from the word, 'The elder shall serve the younger.'"

"*Have you had a crook in your lot?*" "Yes." "*In your health?*" "Yes." "*In your calling?*" "Yes: one disappointment followed another."

"What kept your soul at peace in the midst of it all?" "The sunshine of the covenant."

"*Has your house been as prosperous as you wished; your family—your friends?*" "No; my house is not so with God—he has not made it to grow as I expected. But I remember Whitefield's experience. He had a son whom he expected to become a very extraordinary man, but the son soon died, and his father was cured of his mistake."

"*Have you had affliction in your family?*" "Yes," the dying saint would say, "I tasted the bitterness of grief for a first-born, and the loss of one loved one after another left me like a branchless tree stript and bare. But Jesus was very near in the night of weeping. The sunshine of the everlasting covenant dispelled the gloomy cloud."

"In all these things we are more than conquerors through him that loved us." Clouds of sin, and care, and woe, wrap our sky for a season, but the sun is behind, and the clouds vanish forever as we approach the land of of everlasting day.

Would you have this covenant as your solace, my friend, in a dying hour? Take hold of it now. Close with its blessed proposals. Let it be all your salvation, and all your desire. Cling the more firmly to it as you journey onward and homeward. And when flesh and heart fail, God will be the strength of your heart, and your portion forever.

>"A little while!"—
> And earth shall pass,
> Like a faint vision, from our weary gaze,
> And we shall stand upon the sea of glass,
>   For evermore!
>
> "A little while!"—
> And death shall be,
> With Satan, vanquished at Jehovah's feet,
> And we shall see our Saviour, eye to eye,
>   For evermore!
>
> "A little while!"—
> And every grief
> Shall be remembered, but with tears of joy:
> On Jesus' bosom we shall find relief,
>   For evermore!
>
> "A little while!"—
> And parted hands
> Shall clasp again upon the heavenly shore
> Where she—"*Jerusalem the Golden*"—stands
>   For evermore!

SCHOLA CRUCIS — SCHOLA LUCIS. (*Luther.*)

IV.

THE UNKNOWN WAY AND THE KNOWN GUIDE.

Isaiah xlii. 16.

"And I will bring the blind by a way that they knew not; I will lead them in paths that they have not known: I will make darkness light before them, and crooked things straight. These things will I do unto them, and not forsake them."

THIS chapter is written to help young pilgrims in the narrow way. It is chiefly intended for those who have recently been led to follow Jesus. The writer is a companion in tribulation. He has felt the truth of what he says. He knows the pain of cut feet and broken bones. But he "has something good to say about the narrow way." And as Mr. Ready-to-Halt in Bunyan lent Mr. Feeble-Mind one of his crutches, these words may prove a crutch to some pilgrim who is now going and weeping. A traveller crossing an Alpine pass will learn lessons that may be useful to future travellers.

You have observed that a blind man with a staff in his hand walks pretty confidently along a familiar road; but when he comes to a part of the road that he does not know, his step is slow and cautious. God promises here to "bring the blind by a way that they knew *not*." He deals very tenderly with the blind. The infant in the family is fed first. The sickly child is watched with constant tenderness. The broken limb is softly swathed, and nursed by gentle applications. For the same reasons you find all over the Bible that our Father reserves his choicest mercies for the poor, the sorrowful, the weary, the halt, the blind. Jesus' first words on the Mount were these—"Blessed are the poor in spirit: Blessed are they that mourn."

Observe two general principles.

It could not be expected that we should know the way to heaven of ourselves. It is not to be wondered at that we need to be guided at every step as a blind man along the road. You must know the place before you can know the way to it. You must know the sphere before you can know the training necessary for it. But it doth not yet appear what we shall be. If you do not know the process by which a diamond is polished ere it sparkles in the sovereign's crown, how can you know the process by which a soul is polished to shine in the Saviour's crown forever? If you are ignorant of the usages of earthly courts, and what is fitting in order to appear there, how much more of the preparation necessary for walking with Christ in white in the New Jerusalem! It is quite natural, then, that if we are on the way to the kingdom, we should be like the blind in a way that they know not. Moses felt himself so ignorant of the way to the Promised Land that he prayed—"If thy presence go not with us, carry us not up hence."

It could not be expected that God's manner of leading in the way would be what we think. His ways are higher than our ways, and his thoughts than our thoughts. The God who is from everlasting to everlasting, who fills all space, and reigns in majesty above all worlds, does not see nor act like the blind creatures of a day in anything. His sovereignty challenges a latitude. He moves in a pillar of cloud and of fire even when he guides us to glory. We cannot often interpret his dealings. At every step he says, "What I do thou knowest not now, but thou shalt know hereafter." His way is in the sea, and his path in the great waters, and his footsteps are not known.

We shall consider *The Unknown Way and the Known Guide.*

I. The *Unknown Way.*

God *has* led his people in all ages by a way that they knew not. And, as the finest fabrics are longest in the purifying process, the brightest saints have been led farthest off their course. Take three examples. God promised to make Abraham a great nation, and give him Canaan as his inheritance. He left his country not knowing whither he went; he lived in a strange country without a foot of land except a burial-place; his life was waning away before

Isaac was born—that same Isaac he was called to offer up as a burnt-offering—and it was more than four hundred years before his posterity entered the Promised Land. Look at Jacob. A solitary wanderer, persecuted by an angry brother, wounded by the sins and crimes of his children, his trials followed each other like waves. Joseph, the son of his old age, is sold into Egypt; the great famine comes; his sons go down to Egypt for bread; Simeon is detained in prison; Benjamin is sent for: and the gray-haired, heart-broken saint cries at last, "Me have ye bereaved of my children; Joseph is not, and Simeon is not, and ye will take Benjamin away. All these things are against me." And yet these were the steps that brought him into Joseph's presence. See Joseph clasping his father, and weeping on his neck! Once more. Look at Job, of whom God thrice said that there was none like him in the earth. Hardly ever was saint overwhelmed by such an avalanche of sorrow. He lost his flocks, his herds, and his ten children in one day. Satan smote him with sore bodily disease. Stripped of all, the cup of his bitterness filled to the brim, tempted by his wife, wounded by the hard speeches of heart-whole, unfeeling, coldly-orthodox friends, this pattern of patience cursed his day! Each of these would have said, "What a labyrinth have I passed through!" "Thou broughtest us into the net: thou laidst affliction upon our loins: thou hast caused men to ride over our heads: we went through fire and through water, but thou broughtest us out into a wealthy place. (Ps. lxvi. 11, 12.)

1. *It is by a way unknown that you are brought to Jesus.* This is a great mystery; but I speak of the regeneration of the soul. "The wind bloweth where it listeth, and thou hearest the sound thereof, but canst not tell whence it cometh, and whither it goeth: so is every one that is born of the Spirit." Who can tell the secret of the wind's motion, how it swells from the gentle breeze to the hurricane gust, and then dies away? Who can tell how the grass grows, and the seed ripens, how the magnet draws the iron, and the needle turns to the pole, and the poison in time of pestilence steals

through the air unseen? So secret is the work of the Spirit. Unseen he comes, unseen he departs. Sometimes as the balmy breath of the south wind, sometimes as the stormy blast of the north. When he gently breathes, as he does whenever Christ crucified is set forth, you heed him not—as you do not heed the breath that fans your cheek; but when he comes like a rushing mighty wind, when thousands are bowed down, as on the day of Pentecost, like forest trees bending to the blast, before his divine and awful influence, you cry, "Men and brethren, what shall I do?" Chalmers once preached in Kilmany from John iii. 16: "For God so loved the world, that he gave his only-begotten Son, that whosoever believeth in him should not perish, but have everlasting life." "Did you feel anything strange in church to-day?" said Alexander Paterson to his friend Robert Edie, at the close of the sermon, as they found themselves alone on the road. "I never," he continued, "felt myself undone till to-day as I was listening to that sermon." "It's very strange," said the other, "for it was just the same with me." The two entered a wood close by, and there, unseen by any eye but God's, consecrated themselves to his service. Truly it is by a way that we know not that we are brought to Jesus. These two on their knees in that lone wood have entered in at the strait gate; and all the account they can give of it is, "Did you feel anything strange in church to-day?"

And so with thousands. Your sins are set before you. You feel yourself a child of wrath. Sinai's thunder is exceeding long and loud; and you say, "I exceedingly fear and quake." You thought the day of judgment was come, and all your hopes perished. "I was alive without the law once; but when the commandment came, sin revived and I died." And then Jesus laid his right hand upon you and said, "Come unto me all ye that labor and are heavy-laden, and I will give you rest." With unutterable joy you cast yourself at his feet. But who can tell the mysterious steps by which the soul is led from the moment of its first seeking after him till it rejoices in conscious acceptance?

What was the beginning of it all? Perhaps you have had serious impressions from your earliest years. A mother's tears fell on your cheeks as she told of a Saviour's love. "There was a Face that came through your childish dreams with its mute appealing: there is a voice, a presence, which hath been with you all your days, and which, however you went away from it, starts up ever and again before you, and would not leave you alone." (Memorials of Andrew Crichton, p. 118.) What brought it to a crisis? A remark you heard at the weekly lecture, a tear you saw gathering in the Sabbath-school teacher's eye, the sudden death of a school companion, an illness which brought you to the verge of the grave. The entrance at the strait gate is a way that we know not.

2. *God's dealings with the soul after it is brought to Jesus, both in providence and grace, are as paths unknown.*

There was a law among the Jews, that when a man married he was allowed for a year to enjoy the quiet repose of his home—he was not asked to go out to war; but when the year expired he was included in the regular conscription, and had to face the foe like his neighbors. Exactly similar is the experience of the soul that is newly espoused to the Lord Jesus. He reveals his wonderful glory, and you lay your head upon his breast. "The peace of God, which passeth all understanding," fills your soul. "I cannot have more peace," said Simeon of Cambridge. Gurnall in his "Christian Armor" observes, that Christ's blood was warm in the veins of the early martyrs. So it is with you. Your soul brims over with holy gladness. You sing like Miriam and the rest of the jubilant host when they saw Pharaoh and his captains dead on the shore. You say, "I'll not live long; I'll soon reach the land of Beulah; I'll soon be away from this vexing world, and join the Church of the first-born above." Not a sermon but you go, wet or dry, to hear it. How constant in meditation and prayer! How thirstily you drink the sincere milk of the word! How joyful your Sabbaths! Your soul is fragrant as the rose in spring, and you say, "Oh, if this would last always!" You think that your path to glory is to be smooth and straight and joyful, and that you can go singing all the way.

But suddenly you come to Marah's bitter waters. This is something different from all you have known during the first years of your pilgrim life. There is a cloud on your sky. You hope it will pass away; but you are disappointed. It spreads and spreads, until you lose sight of the sun, and the path, and the triumphant scene behind, and the joyful prospect before. The path becomes unknown and dark and crooked. It becomes strewn with the flint, the brier, and the thorn. And you hear with amazement that enemies whom you had never seen—Canaanites having iron chariots—are in the way before you, ready for battle, and that you must wrestle "not only with flesh and blood, but with principalities and powers, with the rulers of the darkness of this world, and with spiritual wickedness in high places." "To arms! to arms!" is the call of the great Captain of your salvation. "Fight the good fight of faith, lay hold on eternal life." You begin to learn that the Christian life is a pilgrimage through a howling wilderness, a race where the runner must strain every nerve to the end, a voyage over a sea where millions have been shipwrecked, a battle with enemies so desperate that you must either kill or be killed. "Experience is a good teacher, but the fees are heavy." In these circumstances, many a young pilgrim cries in sore perplexity, "This is very different from what my early experience led me to expect!" It may be so: and yet, brother, it is in accordance with the law of the kingdom to which you are journeying — "Through much tribulation we must enter into the kingdom of God;" and it is in accordance with the history of its glorified inhabitants—"These are they who came out of great tribulation."

II. The *Known Guide*.

This is the more welcome part of the subject. Blessed are they that know the joyful sound. Here is a guide who knows the way thoroughly, who will pay all the costs of the journey, who will conquer all your enemies, and who will never leave nor forsake you. In other words, here is a *wise* guide, a *rich* guide, a *strong* guide, and a *loving* guide.

1. A *wise* Guide.—When the Israelites crossed the sea, and saw Pharaoh and his host dead on its shores, and raised the triumphant shout, "Sing unto the Lord, for he hath triumphed gloriously; the horse and his rider hath he thrown into the sea"—had you asked, When do you expect to reach the promised land? "In eleven days," they would have answered. (Deut. i. 2.) Had you asked thirty years afterwards, When do you expect to reach the promised land now? they would have answered, "It is only he who goeth before us in the pillar of cloud and of fire who knows whether we shall ever enter it!" God led them about, but he kept them as the apple of his eye.

Dark and crooked as the way may seem to you, he knows it thoroughly. He has guided a multitude which none can number to Canaan already. He led them forth by the right way. He offers to guide you. He knows the way which is best for you. He puts his word as a staff in your hand. He gives it as a lamp for your feet, and as a light for your path. He offers to guide you with his eye. He wishes you to walk in his light, and not in your own. The pilgrim, after leaving the City of Destruction, would like to some extent to be his own guide. He has some preconceived plans of his own. He would wish a smooth path; God guides him by a rough one. He would wish a short path; God guides him by a circuitous one. He would wish an easy path; God leads him up the Hill Difficulty. He would wish a public path; God guides him by an obscure one. He would wish a safe path; God guides him through a great and terrible wilderness, where there are scorpions, lions' dens, and mountains of leopards. Fellow-pilgrim! God crosses your desires, breaks your plans in pieces, and often appears as if standing with a drawn sword in your way. The promise and the providence cross each other, and sometimes in lines so intricate, that you cannot see the end of it. This is to try and humble and purify you, in order that at last you may be crowned with glory. Oh, let patience have her perfect work! The crooked will be found in the long-run to have been really straight. The darkest spots in your journey will be the brightest, when heaven flashes back its glorious light upon them. We are sure to err if we walk by our own light, and criticise God's ways. He can make your weakness strength, your loss gain, your fall a victory; he can make the crooked straight, darkness light, and death life. Stephen's death helped to spread the gospel. Paul's imprisonment helped to spread the gospel. If John Bunyan had not pined in Bedford jail for twelve years, we had never seen the *Pilgrim's Progress*. If we could learn patience from the boy who met with a sore accident, and silenced the friends who mourned over his broken leg by saying, "God never made a mistake!" The sweetest mercy God ever gave you will yet be found to be, that he brought you by a way that you knew not.

2. A *rich* Guide.—See the provision he has made for the refreshment of pilgrims by the way. He has provided resting-places—green

spots like Elim—and in these he has stored wine and milk, manna from heaven, and honey out of the rock. He brings pilgrims to his banqueting-house. He anoints their heads with oil. He makes their cup run over. He gives them earnests of Canaan. The Interpreter's house, and the arbor in the brow of the Hill Difficulty, and the Beautiful Palace, and Gaius' house, and the walk along the banks of the river of God, and the shepherds' tents on the Delectable Mountains, and the joys of the land of Beulah —these set forth the riches of the guide. The very poverty of the pilgrims is a mirror in which we may see his riches. He has a salve for every wound of theirs, and a cordial for every sorrow. He has a pardon for every sin, and a fulness for every want. It pleased the Father that in him should all fulness dwell. The saints' bills are paid at first sight, whatever the amount is.

View it thus. The saints in glory are a multitude which none can number. How bright these glorious spirits shine! They were once wretched and miserable, and poor, and blind, and naked. And yet every one of them has been blessed with *all* spiritual blessings in heavenly places in Christ. Every one of them has received pardon for countless sins and supplies of grace in countless trials. We are lost in the thought. Our guide is as rich as ever. He is able to do exceeding abundantly above all that you can ask or think.

Fellow-pilgrim! Think of that one word—"The unsearchable riches of Christ." The ocean whose waters surround the world, and fill all its lakes and rivers, is a type of the riches of your guide. Who can exhaust the ocean? The grandest type of all is the sun, that for six thousand years has poured his floods of light, that continues to shine unexhausted, and conveys life, and light, and heat, to unnumbered millions. But no type can fully represent the unsearchable riches. Behold the unsearchable riches of Christ revealed in the gospel—the riches of his merit—the riches of his love—the riches of his grace—the riches of his consolations! When the famine waxed sore in Egypt, Pharaoh had but one advice to the starving multitudes, "Go to Joseph!" Joseph opened the store-houses and sold to the Egyptians. O that dying sinners flocked to Christ's open store-houses as these starving Egyptians flocked to Joseph! O that there were a run upon the Bank of free grace! What joy would it create in heaven!

3. A *strong* Guide.—Close to my father's house a beautiful wood covered to the top a steep hill that rose out of a quiet lake. The road passed through the wood. As a child, I never took this road alone in the dark without being afraid. My father was a strong, powerful man. When he held my hand, I could walk fearlessly through the wood in the darkest night. All the idle fears of spirits of the wood and wraiths of the water that haunted the child's mind melted away when his father walked beside him and smiled at his fears.

Pilgrim! many of your fears are as unfounded as the fears of childhood. You walk in darkness, and a stone seems a lion, a friend seems an enemy, the right way seems the wrong. The cure for your fears is to keep near your guide. Pray that he would take you by the hand. Tell him your fears. Study the "Fear Nots" of the Bible—"Fear not, for I am with thee:" "It is I, be not afraid:" "Fear not, little flock"—and your fears will melt away.

He is a strong guide. He can carry all your burdens. And if you cannot walk, he will carry yourself. "The eternal God is thy refuge, and underneath are the everlasting arms."

He can conquer all your enemies. He triumphed over them on the cross. "Be of good cheer," he says, "I have overcome the world." He took the sting of death away. Death quails before him. Devils tremble for fear of him. And oh! he can kill sin within you. He can strangle the scorpions that bite you. "The God of peace shall bruise Satan under your feet shortly." "The Egyptians whom ye have seen to-day, ye shall see them again no more forever." "Thou shalt tread upon the lion and the adder: the dragon and the young lion shalt thou trample under foot." No wonder that Ralph Erskine, as his end drew near, uttered the joyful shout, "Victory, victory, through the blood of the Lamb!" No wonder that a venerable saint, who lately died in the Lord, said in his last moments, "The shadows of death are falling over me, but I am going to my great Elder Brother in the heavens!"

4. A *loving* Guide.—"These things will I do unto them, and not forsake them." He loves you as the apple of his eye. He loves you too well to give you your good things in this world. He loves you too well to let you be puffed up with pride. "Can a woman forget her sucking child, that she should not have compassion on the son of her womb? yea, she may forget, yet will I not forget thee." But he puts crooks in your lot. It is love. He leads you in a way that you know not. It is love. He lets trials in your person, business, family, come rolling over you like waves. It is love. He hides his face from you. It is love. He empties you from vessel to vessel. It is love. He puts you in a fiery furnace. It is love. "There's not one drop of wrath in all this," said a godly woman when dying in great bodily agony. The molten gold is more precious to the refiner than the

bullion. Study, then, the actings of this love; for it *is* hard for a child to believe that the physician loves him when he cuts off the incurable limb. A *loving* guide—and, therefore, these things are certain: No evil shall hurt you; a guard of angels shall watch around you; all providences shall work together for your good; and, best of all, the Guide himself will stand at the top of the ladder, and give you the best wine at the last. "Well done, good and faithful servant: enter thou into the joy of thy Lord." Oh, happy pilgrim, though foolish, with such a wise guide! happy though poor, with such a rich guide! happy though weak, with such a strong guide! happy though desolate, with such a loving guide! Behold, a guide who will redeem you, pardon you, seal you, guide you, guard you—a guide who will never leave you, who will hold up your head in crossing the Jordan, and take you to his throne in heaven!

"And when I'm to die,
Receive me, I'll cry;
For Jesus hath loved me,
I cannot tell why.

> "But this I do find,
> That we two are so joined,
> Christ will not be in glory,
> And leave me behind."

This may fall into the hands of some pilgrim who has long followed the Lamb, and does not yet enjoy the fulfilment of this promise. My brother! your feeling is, "My darkness is not yet made light, and the crooked lines in my experience are as crooked as ever." But wait the issue. Wait until you "see the end of the Lord." Remember the words of Jesus to Martha, "Said I not unto thee that if thou wouldest believe, thou shouldest see the glory of God?" As surely as Joseph's promotion casts a radiance back on his woes in the dungeon, so will it be with you. It will be part of heaven's joy to look back and see how really straight was the seemingly crooked. The "blind" are often led on and up till at last they land in glory, and then begins the wonder, "Oh, have all my crosses and heartbreaks, all my crooked experiences, all my sighs and tears, come to this! Have all these rough blasts blown me to this happy shore!

But some will read this who are without Christ as their guide. They walk in the way of their hearts, and in the sight of their eyes. Dear friend! you need a guide. The way is unknown. It is dark and slippery. A guide is indispensable. Oh, will you not choose this guide now? The writer never felt the value of a guide so much as once when crossing a glacier. A glacier is a river of ice. The blue ice rising and falling like frozen waves, the fearful crevasses gaping here and there, the slippery path, where every second step is cut in the ice; woe to the traveller who tries to cross without a guide. Christless soul! your path is far more slippery, and your danger far greater. It is a sore death to fall into a crevasse, or to plunge down an ice precipice; but a sorer death will be his who, refusing Jesus' blessed guidance, stumbles in sin's slippery road, and falls into the pit wherein is no water.

V.

REMEMBERING ALL THE WAY.

DEUT. viii. 2-5, 16.

"And thou shalt remember all the way which the Lord thy God led thee these forty years in the wilderness, to humble thee, and to prove thee, to know what was in thine heart, whether thou wouldest keep his commandments or no. And he humbled thee, and suffered thee to hunger, and fed thee with manna. . . . Thy raiment waxed not old upon thee, neither did thy foot swell, these forty years. . . . As a man chasteneth his son, so the Lord thy God chasteneth thee. . . . To do thee good at thy latter end."

IN beginning life we look forward, and people the future with bright visions. As life advances the tendency is to look backward; and very impressive is the contrast between the high hopes of the boy and the sober experience of the man. A great writer observes, that the distant "rainbow seems to be a real arch of emerald and gold; its limb rests on the side of the hill—you climb and find nothing but damp mist :" so the rainbow hopes of early life vanish before the stern lessons of after years. In beginning the Christian life, too, the mind is full of happy dreams, which are corrected by riper experience. The early aspirations of the closet are strangely qualified by the realities of the subsequent life. This is beautifully illustrated by Israel's history in the wilderness. The wilderness was a school in which God trained them for forty years. Every day was full of a most impressive discipline. When they entered this school—when they sang their song of triumph beside the Sea—they expected a speedy victory over their enemies, and a joyful entrance into the Promised Land. But God had great lessons to teach them, and before they could learn these it was necessary that they should continue in the wilderness a long season. So the Christian life is a school in which God trains us for heaven.

It is stated thrice in this chapter that the special end of the discipline in the wilderness was to *humble* Israel. (Ver. 2, 3, 16.) Pride is the strongest root in our nature—pride of our works, prayers, tears—yea, even of our humility. Though extirpated in one place, it will sprout forth in another: "Like the fabled monsters of old from whose dissevered neck the blood sprang forth, and formed fresh heads." It must die many deaths. It took forty years to teach Israel to be humble. Hezekiah, the Reformer king, fell into pride in the matter of the Babylonian ambassadors. Baruch never had so hard a lesson to learn as this—"Seekest thou great things for thyself, seek them not." It is easy to speak of humility: it is easy to say that it is the loveliest of the graces, that it resembles the blushing lily, and that pride is the condemnation of the devil; but to crucify pride—to cast down high imaginations, and bring every thought into captivity to the obedience of Christ—to slay self, self-righteousness, self-importance, self-seeking, self-pleasing—to adopt with meek tears the motto, "Christ is all, and Self is nothing,"—is an achievement which flesh and blood cannot perform, but the power of the

Holy Ghost. It often takes forty years' severe discipline to attain to this.

God humbles man by showing him *what is in his heart.* "To know what is in thine heart." Had God led Israel at once into the Promised Land, they would never have known themselves. In the song which thrilled on Miriam's harp, there is not a note which betrays the unbelief of the chosen people—their murmuring, their rebellion, their idolatry in Horeb—their loathing of the manna—their contempt of the pleasant land. But the wilderness tried them. A mother teaches her babe to walk by letting its feeble limbs bend under it. It gets many a fall, but she contrives that it shall fall in her arms. Thus God suffers his saints to be tempted, and even to fall into sin, in order to teach them what is in their hearts; but he keeps his everlasting arms underneath them. The sad falls of David and Peter were permitted to show that the root of every sin remains in the renewed heart. We do not know ourselves till the stress of temptation comes. John Newton frankly confesses that in the warmth of his early discipleship he expected to be sanctified *brevi manu;* but that is not God's way.

> "I hoped that in some favored hour,
>   At once he'd answer my request;
> And by his love's constraining power,
>   Subdue my sins, and give me rest.
>
> "Instead of this, he made me feel
>   The hidden evils of my heart:
> And let the angry powers of hell
>   Assault my soul in every part.
>
> "Yea, more, with his own hand he seemed
>   Intent to aggravate my woe:
> Crossed all the fair designs I schemed,
>   Blasted my gourds, and laid me low.
>
> "'Lord, why is this?' I trembling cried.
>   'Wilt thou pursue thy worm to death?'
> ''Tis in this way,' the Lord replied,
>   'I answer prayer for grace and faith.
>
> "'These inward trials I employ,
>   From self and pride to set thee free;
> And break thy schemes of earthly joy,
>   That thou mayest seek thy all in me.'"

In treating this subject there are two courses open to us:

First, To review the chief resting-places where Israel halted. This would lead us, in the wake of the pillar of cloud, to taste of Marah's bitter waters, and to the refreshing shade of

Elim's palm-trees. It would lead us to the desert of sin, where God rained down the manna, and to Rephidim, where the water gushed from the rock. It would lead us to Sinai with its blackness and darkness and tempest, and to the wilderness of Paran, where Moses said to Hobab, "We are journeying to the place of which the Lord said, I will give it you; come thou with us and we will do thee good." It would lead us by the land of Edom, where Moses lifted up the brazen serpent, and by the plains of Moab, where Balaam saw Israel in their glittering tents. It would lead us to Mount Hor, where Aaron died, and to Mount Nebo, from whose summit Moses looked across upon the Promised Land. This might be a very profitable mode of treatment. We might glean many full ears in so rich a portion of the Kinsman's field: or—

Second, To consider the characteristics of God's guidance all through the wilderness.

We shall take the second of these methods. And there are four characteristics of God's guidance which we shall reverently consider.

It was *sovereign, mysterious, fatherly,* and *all-wise.*

1. It was *Sovereign.* God is a great King. "He does according to his will in the armies of heaven, and among the inhabitants of the earth." Sovereignty belongs to the very idea of God. Cherubim and seraphim cast their crowns at his feet. You see his sovereignty in *creation.* "He spake and it was done, he commanded and it stood fast." The archangel and the worm, the atom that floats in the breeze and the sun that shines in the firmament, arose from nothing at his word. You see it in *Providence.* It binds the sweet influences of Pleiades and looses the bands of Orion, and at the same moment guides the fall of a sparrow. It shapes our destinies. It fixes the bounds of our habitations. "There's a divinity that shapes our ends, rough-hew them as we will." One takes to merchandise—another to books—another to politics—and they imagine that their own wills have so ordained it. As well might the fly on the carriage-wheel exclaim, "What a dust do I raise," as worms of the dust attrib-

ute to their own foresight those movements which are ordained by him who hath of old prepared his throne in the heavens, and whose kingdom ruleth over all. God moves behind the dial-plate, and the touch of his finger regulates the wondrous mechanism of the universe. When the ship is sailing over the pathless sea, some of the passengers may be walking forward, some aft, some may be standing still, and some sleeping securely in their berths; but the man at the helm controls the movements of them all as he steers his ship through the billows.

You see the same sovereignty in *grace*. "I thank thee, O Father, Lord of heaven and earth, because thou hast hid these things from the wise and prudent, and hast revealed them unto babes." God showed his sovereignty in choosing Israel from among the nations. He showed it in guiding them through the wilderness. He taught them that his will and not theirs must be their rule. They must bow their heads and adore. Like a tall angel beckoning, the pillar of cloud led the way, and they must follow. It often moved by night when they would wish it to rest, and it often rested by day when they wished it to move. Sometimes it went backwards. But they must follow it. Their safety —their very life—depended on this.

How sovereign the Divine guidance has been in *your own* case! Remember the day when he brought you out of Egypt, and led you through the Red Sea. Remember the day when he separated you from your old companions. You were no better than they. Perhaps you were worse. But grace laid hold of you.

> "Chosen not for good in me,
> Wakened up from wrath to flee."

Bunyan tells, in his Grace Abounding, that when a boy he had a narrow escape from drowning. Soon after, he enlisted in the Parliamentary army. His regiment being ordered to the siege of Leicester, he repented of the step he had taken, and got a comrade to take his place. His comrade was shot through the head. A loose woman in the street rebuked him for swearing, and told him that he was the most fearful swearer she had ever heard, and that he was enough to corrupt the whole town. After many sore struggles, he "came up to the Cross, and his burden loosed from off his shoulders, and fell from his back, and began to tumble, and so continued to do, till it came to the mouth of the sepulchre, where it fell in and he saw it no more."

Perhaps the lines in your case are not so clear. Still you can remember that, when God began to deal with you, you were as clay in the hands of the potter. You can see that a Higher Power than your own ordained the circumstances which resulted in your conversion. You can recall the prayers of a mother now in heaven. You can recall the book that first made you feel that you had a soul. Perhaps it was "The Saint's Rest," or "The Dairyman's Daughter," or "The Anxious Inquirer," or "The Sinner's Friend." You can recall the sermon which you could not forget—the word which left an indelible mark upon your heart—the starting tear—the spot where first you sought to be alone with God. And possibly you met an old companion who confessed that he felt as you felt. Or you can recall the illness that brought you to the edge of the grave, or the bereavement that left such a wasteful blank in the house. There may be much darkness in your spiritual conceptions—you may seldom be able to say with full assurance, "One thing I know, that whereas I was blind, now I see;"—but, my friend, you can never forget your first sight of the Cross, your first sense of pardon, your first sacrament, when Jesus stood unveiled to faith in his person and love and death, and you plighted your troth in the words, "What things were gain to me, those I counted loss for Christ; yea doubtless, and I count all things but loss for the excellency of the knowledge of Christ Jesus my Lord, for whom I have suffered the loss of all things, and do count them but dung that I may win Christ!"

Grace and love appear in all these steps; but it is the grace and love of the King of kings. Who made you to differ? Why were you taken when others were left? It was *sovereign* grace. But remember God is as sovereign in ordering the subsequent steps of the pilgrimage as in ordering the earlier ones. If we kept this in mind, it would teach us child-like, unquestioning submission. "Not as I will, but as thou wilt." Charnocke observes, in his great work on the Attributes, that "if we lose sight of God's sovereignty we fall into error, just as in a school, if the master is out of sight, the children leave their places, and the school is in confusion." A right apprehension of God's sovereignty is not only the best safeguard against theological error, but the best safeguard against fretting and murmuring. The young disciple has an ideal which he hopes to reach, a work which he hopes to do—he has favorite plans and schemes which, it may be, have cost him many a prayer:—but as he advances in the Christian life, and sees the great wheel of Providence breaking his plans in pieces, and scattering his hopes like withered leaves—he learns the deeper truth, "There are many devices in a man's heart; nevertheless the counsel of the Lord, that shall stand." (Prov. xix. 21.)

> "Thy way, not mine, O Lord,
> However dark it be!

> Lead me by thine own hand,
> Choose out the path for me.
>
> "Smooth let it be or rough,
> It will be still the best;
> Winding or straight, it leads
> Right onward to thy rest."

2. It was *mysterious*.

"It is the glory of God to conceal a thing." "Clouds and darkness are round about him, righteousness and judgment are the habitation of his throne." We could not bear the insufferable splendor of his presence,—therefore in mercy to us "he maketh darkness his secret place, his pavilion round about him are dark waters and thick clouds of the skies." The mysteriousness of his guidance was fitly emblemed by the pillar of cloud, which in one respect revealed God, but in another concealed him. The same lesson is taught in Ezekiel's vision of the wheels—where, to show in the same breath the incomprehensibleness and the unerring wisdom of God's counsels, it is said, "The rings were so high that they were dreadful, and they were full of eyes round about them four." (Ezek. i. 18.)

How strangely light and shade alternated in their history. Their forty years were like an April day—sunshine and shower. A great deliverance, then murmuring; Marah, then Elim; hunger, then angels' food; thirst, then the rock turned into a fountain of waters; Sinai's thunder, then peace through the sprinkling of blood; fear, then victory; weariness, then Rest: such was the history of the chosen people in the wilderness. Such is their history now. It must be so. It is only children that ask, Why does the tide ebb and flow—why are there waves on the sea—why are there clouds on the sky? "While the earth remaineth, *summer* and *winter*, and *day* and *night*, shall not cease." The Christian life is a series of ups and downs. What alternations of grief and gladness! To-day in the banqueting-house, to-morrow eating the bread of tears. To-day coming up from the wilderness leaning on your Beloved, to-morrow walking in darkness. To-day in a large room, to-morrow without a place where to plant your feet. To-day on Pisgah breathing the air of heaven, to-morrow breathing the *malaria* of earth. Faint yet pursuing, sorrowful yet always rejoicing, cast down and lifted up, wounded and healed, weakened and strengthened, emptied and filled, allied to heaven by reason of the new man, allied to hell by reason of the old man, tempted by the devil, defended by the Omnipotent arm of him who came to destroy the works of the devil: behold the many-sided discipline of the family of God. "And it shall come to pass in that day, that the light shall not be clear, nor dark: but it shall be one day which shall be known to the Lord, not day, nor night; but it shall come to pass, that at evening time it shall be light." (Zech. xiv. 6, 7.) It shall not be clear sunshine, nor total darkness, but a dim twilight, as you journey onwards and upwards. But it shall be one day—a day altogether *unique*, different from all others—which shall be known to the Lord; and it shall brighten gloriously towards evening.*

* This is powerfully put by Mr. Spurgeon: "A pilgrim sets out in the morning, and he has to journey many a day before he gets to the shrine which he seeks. What varied scenes the traveller will behold on his way! Sometimes he

How strangely God made all things work together for their good.

A ship on her voyage to Madeira was caught in a storm, and in danger of being lost. A godly minister on board prayed for calm weather, and his prayer was answered. They had a fortnight of calm, without a breath of wind. They soon found, however, that this was very

will be on the mountains, anon he will descend into the valleys; here he will be where the brooks shine like silver, where the birds warble, where the air is balmy, and the trees are green, and luscious fruits hang down to gratify his taste: anon he will find himself in the arid desert, where no life is found, and no sound is heard, except the screech of the wild eagle in the air: where he finds no rest for the sole of his foot—the burning sky above him, and the hot sand beneath him— no roof-tree and no house to rest himself: at another time he finds himself in a sweet oasis, resting himself by the wells of water, and plucking fruit from palm-trees. One moment he walks between the rocks in some narrow gorge, where all is darkness: at another time he ascends the hill Mizar: now he descends into the valley of Baca; anon he climbs the hill of Bashan,—'a high hill is the hill of Bashan;' and yet again going into the den of leopards, he suffers trial and affliction. Such is the Christian life— ever changing. Who can tell what may come next? To-day it is fair—the next day there may be the thundering storm; to-day I may want for nothing—to-morrow I may be like Jacob, with nothing but a stone for my pillow, and the heavens for my curtains. But what a happy thought it is,

undesirable, for during the whole fortnight they scarcely made a single mile of way. In the storm they had been running fast before the wind under bare poles. They had to pray for wind again. It is thus that God uses the storm of temptation to drive us on our voyage. In the calm we make no progress.

A gentleman on a visit to a friend saw a beautiful horse feeding about in the pasture with a clog on his foot, and asked, "Why do you clog such a noble animal?" "Sir," said he, "I would a great deal sooner clog him than lose him; he is given to leaping hedges." That is the reason why God clogs his people. He would rather clog them than lose them; for if he did not clog them, they would leap the

though we know not where the road winds, we know where it ends. It is the straightest way to heaven to go round about. Israel's forty years wanderings were, after all, the nearest path to Canaan. We may have to go through trial and affliction: the pilgrimage may be a tiresome one, but it is safe: we cannot trace the river upon which we are sailing, but we know it ends in floods of bliss at last. We cannot track the roads, but we know that they all meet in the great metropolis of heaven, in the centre of God's universe."— *Spurgeon.*

hedges and be gone. They want a tether to prevent them from straying.

My friend! remember all the way which the Lord led thee. "The great and terrible wilderness, the fiery serpents and scorpions and drought" (ver. 15), the hunger and thirst, were all designed to *do thee good at thy latter end.* Sickness, bereavement, tears, want, woe, disappointments, hidings, doubts, fears—are the ingredients in the medicine which the Physician employs to cure your ail. You may not see *how* it is so. Believe that it is so. He can make seemingly contrary providences conspire for this end,—just as the wheels of a watch, though moving in contrary directions, have all one end —the regulation of time. "Remember all the way which the Lord led thee,"—until, lost in wonder, love, and praise, you sing, "As the heavens are higher than the earth, so are his ways higher than our ways, and his thoughts than our thoughts."

> "With mercy and with judgment,
> My web of time he wove,
> And aye the dews of sorrow
> Were lustred with his love.

> I'll bless the hand that guided,
> I'll bless the heart that planned,
> When throned where glory dwelleth
> In Emmanuel's land." *

And how minute the links on which he hangs the grandest results! One night, when John Wesley was an infant, his father's house took fire. All the inmates escaped, and the good man was in the act of thanking God for their deliverance, when he discovered that the infant was missing. The flames were bursting through the windows, and the crackling roof was almost falling in. At this awful moment the nurse, almost suffocated with smoke and scorched with the flames, was seen standing in the window of the top story, with the infant in her arms, shrieking for help. The father seized a ladder, planted it against the wall, sprang to the top, and saved the child. Another moment, and they had been buried in the ruins. And this was the man—thus saved from the fire—who,

---

* On the wall of the old castle of Huntly, one of the Dukes of Gordon carved the words which may still be read, "TO · THAES · THAT · LOVE · GOD · AL · THINGIS · VIRKIS · FOR · THE · BEST."—*Duchess of Gordon's Life.*

during a ministry of sixty years, approved himself as the holiest and most laborious man of his age—who preached sixty thousand sermons—and gave an unparalleled impulse to the Christianity of England!

3. It was *fatherly*.

"Thou shalt also consider in thine heart, that, as a man chasteneth his son, so the Lord thy God chasteneth thee." (Ver. 5.) "The Lord thy God bare thee, as a man doth bear his son, in all the way that ye went, until ye came into this place." (Deut. i. 31.) In Acts xiii. 18, where we read in the common version, "About the time of forty years suffered he their manners in the wilderness"—the true reading is admitted to be, "He cherished them as a nurse the infant in her bosom." He "bare them as on eagles' wings, and brought them to himself." When they were hungry, he gave them bread from heaven. It fell around their tents. Every day brought a new supply. They had only to gather it. It never failed till they reached Canaan. When they were thirsty, he gave them water from the rock. Their raiment waxed not old, and their shoes never grew old upon their feet for forty years. (Deut. xxix. 5.) When they knew not where to go, he guided them by the cloudy pillar. When they were beset by enemies, he defended them as a wall of fire. It was *fatherly* guidance. When it was severe, it was the severity of Love. "As many as I love, I rebuke and chasten." For forty years he carried them as a father carries a weary or sickly child in his arms.

He has dealt thus with you. He has given you the *true bread* from heaven. You have eaten Christ's flesh, which is meat indeed, and his blood, which is drink indeed. He has fed you with the finest of the wheat, and with honey out of the rock he has satisfied you. Ah, my friend! remember all the way which the Lord thy God led thee these forty years. What manna you have found in the Bible! What hallowed hours you have spent over it, until a glory rested on the page, and its texts shone like stars! Remember communion Sabbaths long ago, when you came to the house of God dark and sad, and a glorious light surprised you, and you went home saying, "I have seen more in the Word to-day than I'll ever be able to express in this world!". Remember the day when God gave the minister the very word that met your case, that healed your wound, and soothed your sorrow, and made you say, "It looks as if some one had told him!" Such words have often come back even in a dying hour, and pillowed the dying head. Boston tells of one of his flock who died in the Lord, and who said to him with his last breath, "I bless God that ever I've seen your face!"

And he has given you *raiment which never grows old*, and shoes which will last till you walk the golden streets. Remember the day when he said, "Bring forth the best robe, and put it on him, and put a ring upon his hand, and shoes on his feet."

Remember how he guided you when you knew not where to go. Remember critical junctures in your history—marked eras, beautifully named "the water-sheds of life," where a false step had been fatal, and no human voice could direct; and when you cried out of the depths of your perplexity, "Lead, Saviour, lead," you "heard a voice behind you saying, This is the way, walk thou in it." How often you have had experience of this!

Remember how he delivered you from your enemies by the way. The archers sorely grieved you. Satan wounded you with his fiery darts, and you were brought low; but he bound up your wounds, and enabled you to say, "Rejoice not against me, O mine enemy: when I fall, I shall arise; when I sit in darkness, the Lord shall be a light unto me." Remember that a Father has been guiding you these forty years in the wilderness.

Two boys wandered from home, and came to a very high tree. They were told that if they climbed to the top they could see very far. One of them tried to climb, but when he was half-way up, the branch broke, and he fell to the ground. His brother, almost dead with fear, tried to lift him, but could not. At last he ran home to tell his father. He was afraid to tell. His heart was too big, and he stammered. His father saw in his face what happened, and cried, "Tell me where my poor bruised boy is!" and ran to help the sufferer. That boy learned more of a father's heart that day than he had known before. My friend, let us deeply ponder the fatherly love of God. We suffer much by forgetting it. Dr. Macdonald of Ferintosh expressed regret on his death-bed that he had not dwelt more in his preaching on the love of the Father.

4. It was *all-wise.*

The best means were used for the best ends. The ends were to humble us and to prove us, to make us know what was in our hearts, and to do us good at the latter end. God's guidance of us was the best fitted to secure these ends.

We cannot see this now—struggling uphill, veiled in mists, often crushed and ill-bestead—but when we reach the summit, and get into the glorious light, we shall see that every part of our discipline, to its minutest details, was indispensable to work us to God's ideal—to make us what he would have us to be. We shall then see how sweet were the uses of adversity. We shall then see that want and woe were blessed angels in disguise. We shall then see that the night of weeping was the time when Christ was nearest and the promises sweetest, as darkness shows us worlds of light we never saw by day. We shall then see that by sending bereavement God but darkened our room to give us clearer visions of his glory. We shall then see that he never once did us an unkind thing. We shall then see that it was in great mercy and love that he refused to answer many of our prayers.* We would shake the tree before the fruit was ripe. He would not *let* us eat unripe fruit. He kept us waiting till the "due season," and in our impatience we "chattered like a crane or a swallow," and thought

---

* "A child who has never seen a serpent before, and who looks at it through the glass frame, may think it very beautiful. As it curls and glides about in its folds of green and gold, and its ruby eyes sparkle in the sun, it looks far prettier than more familiar objects, and the child may long to grasp it. 'But what man is there among you who is a father, if his son ask a serpent, will he give him the serpent?' And supposing that the fretful child should weep because he is not allowed to fondle the asp, could worse befall him than just to be allowed to smash the case and clutch the envenomed reptile?"—*Mount of Olives*, p. 137.

that he dealt out to us very hard lines. We shall then see that "terrible things in righteousness" were the best answer to our prayers. We shall then see that the weariness and painfulness of the wilderness, the straits that pinched us, the crooks in our lot that worried us, and even the falls that often made us give up all for lost—were all needed. There was a "need-be" (1 Pet. i. 6) for them, else he would not have sent them: "for he doth not afflict willingly, nor grieve the children of men: but though he cause grief, yet he will have compassion according to the multitude of his mercies." (Lam. iii. 32, 33.) Captain Cook tells that once in a dark, stormy night, he saw by the glare of a flash of lightning a ship beside him which, but for the flash, he must have run foul of. It was a strange means of deliverance. As strange are many of the ways which God takes to deliver his own, and to do them good in their latter end. "By ten thousand thousand instrumentalities, and agencies, and influences—the circumstances of your infancy; the opportunities, companionships, and temptations of your youth; the trials, occupations, and connections of your riper years, he has been unconsciously forming and fashioning you" into a vessel of honor.* How tender the words, "*to do thee good at thy latter end!*" Remember Israel's experience—"There *failed not aught of any good* thing which the Lord had spoken unto the house of Israel; all came to pass." (Joshua xxi. 45.)

We conclude with three words of counsel to fellow-pilgrims:

First, *Set up a memorial pillar this day*, and call it Ebenezer, saying, "Hitherto hath the Lord helped us." Take a broad and discriminating view of the mercies God has showered upon you these forty years. Muse on them till the fire burns. Cultivate a thankful, joyful, praising spirit. Sing like David, "Who am I, O Lord God, and what is my house that thou hast brought me hitherto:" "What shall I render unto the Lord for all his benefits towards me?" Remember the Bethels, the Peniels, the Elims, the Ebenezers along the way. Look

* Milne's "Gatherings from a Ministry," p. 12.

back and see as many Ebenezers piled up behind you, as there are miles from Dundee to London, with oil poured upon the top of them! Remember the sacred spots, the hallowed hours. Think of this danger and that danger from which he saved you, of this rock and that rock on which you might have made shipwreck. "You know some of your youthful comrades who have gone flagrantly astray. They have dropped from the current and highway of life, and are become outcasts and waifs in society." You are on your way to the Celestial City. He has brought you thus far, and he says to-day, "My presence shall go with thee, and I will give thee rest." All you have got is only a drop of the ocean. The milk and honey are beyond the wilderness. The crown is glittering yonder.

Second, *Mourn over past unprofitableness.* Forty years are a long time to learn a lesson, and it is a bitter thought if the forty years are gone, and the lesson unlearned. Drop a tear over the murmurings of the wilderness. Drop a tear over the sins of your youth, over secret sins, over your besetting sin. Drop a tear over the years which the locust hath eaten. And redouble your diligence, for the time is short.

Third, *Look joyfully forward.* The Christian's golden age is Onward. Those whom God has led these forty years in the wilderness are now near the rest that remaineth. The fact that you have had troubles is a proof of Jesus' faithfulness: for you have had one-half of his legacy already, and you will soon have the other half. (John xvi. 33.) Soon you will sight the shining shore. The ship that has plunged and labored in the midnight tempest will soon be seen with her white sails all spread entering the haven of Emmanuel's Land. Wilberforce has a beautiful thought: "Sailors on their voyage will drink 'Friends astern' till they are half-way over, then 'Friends ahead': with me it has been 'Friends ahead' this long time."

Some can look back on forty or sixty years of wandering in the wilderness who are not pilgrims to Canaan. They have no deliverance from Egypt to look back upon. They have no newbirth-day to look back upon. Life is a wilderness journey to them too—rough and weary—through serpents and scorpions and drought; but alas! with no Canaan beyond. It is the saddest thought in the world. To look back on a lost life—the flower of one's days—the *whole* of one's days given to the service of the devil! My friend, mourn over a wasted life: haste to the door of mercy which is yet standing open, lest God swear in his wrath that you shall not enter into his rest. You have not a moment to lose!

> "God moves in a mysterious way
>   His wonders to perform;
> He plants his footsteps in the sea,
>   And rides upon the storm.
>
> "Ye fearful saints, fresh courage take:
>   The clouds ye so much dread
> Are big with mercy, and shall break
>   In blessings on your head.
>
> "Judge not the Lord by feeble sense,
>   But trust him for his grace;
> Behind a frowning Providence
>   He hides a smiling face.
>
> "His purposes will ripen fast,
>   Unfolding every hour;
> The bud may have a bitter taste,
>   But sweet will be the flower."

NEC VOLENTI—NEC VOLANTI.

VI.

THE STRANGER IN THE EARTH.

Psalm cxix. 19.
"I am a stranger in the earth."

"I am soon to leave this beautiful world, and I am anxious to carry as perfect a calotype of it as possible along with me: and, therefore, I gaze with unwearied delight upon the trees and flowers, and the blue sky and the faces of men."—Rev. Dr. John Duncan.

YOU have seen Knox's monument in the Necropolis of Glasgow. The statue of the great reformer, looking down from its high column, seems to speak words of warning to us still. About fifty yards to the west of this monument, and down the slope of the hill, may be seen a slab in the face of the rock with the two brief texts graven upon it, "Jesus wept;" "Behold the Lamb of God."

Beneath this slab sleeps the dust of a bright little stranger, whose visit to this pilgrim land was very short, and who, as soon as he had learned to lisp the names of father and mother, and the sweet name of Jesus, was taken home to sing the new song. He had learned to join in singing the psalm at our family worship, and each night ere he closed his eyes he had learned to pray :

>"In the kingdom of thy grace
>Grant a little child a place."

He had been once in church, and on the morning of his last Sabbath on earth, the 20th of March, 1859, when a snow-storm kept him at home, he said, as we were leaving for the sanctuary, "Johnnie will pray to God to help papa to preach." The two texts graven on the slab were the two last texts he repeated. His little speeches had such a fascinating interest to our ears that we felt his presence as a blessed sunbeam in the house. And it was hard, after his stay of only two years and four months, suddenly to part with him, and to see his fine manly face and silken hair laid in darkness amid the clods of the churchyard. It made the earth lonelier to us. But it made the grave lightsomer.

He being dead yet speaketh. The parting with so bright a visitant helped to *burn* into the writer's spirit the words, "I am a stranger in the earth." It has led to the writing of this chapter.

Your home has been visited by death. Some of your dearest treasures have been taken from you. We shall not speak of death now. We shall rather speak of present duties and future hopes. A glimpse of the Deathless Land takes the sting of death away. A believing view of the happy meetings on the resurrection morning heals our sorrow for the bitter partings of Earth!

The lesson we wish to open up is, that *the Saint is a Stranger in the Earth.* "I am a stranger in the earth." We shall—

    I. *Give a short exposition of this lesson.*
    II. *Make a short application of it.*

I. THE SHORT EXPOSITION.

"I am a stranger in the earth," means—1. That *the Saint is not born of the earth.* A man is a stranger when he lives far from where he was born. The saint is born from heaven. His name is in the family register of heaven. The new birth makes a world-wide difference between God's children and the world, although it may not be very apparent now. One born on the other side of the globe is a stranger here. He is not like us in complexion, in feature, in dress, in speech, in manner. The negro's dark skin and woolly head, the turban and loose robe of the Asiatic, the broad fair features and deep guttural speech of the German, the dark eyes and Roman contour of the Italian face, the Frenchman's polite and lively ways, mark them out as strangers in our streets. But if one born a thousand miles away is a stranger here, how much more is one born from heaven! He bears the image of the heavenly—the heavenly family likeness. Though in the world, he is not of the world. He is of another race and another kingdom. Jesus was a stranger in the earth. "Ye are from beneath," said he to the Jews; "I am from above: ye are of this world; I am not of this world." So is it with the saint. "As He is, so are we in this world."

2. *The saint is not known on the earth.*

A stranger is one whom we don't know. A stranger in the earth is one whom the world does not know. The world did not know Jesus. It denied his person and mission, his character and work. He was despised and rejected of men. And so "the world knoweth us not, because it knew him not." The world knew David in a sense, and yet it did not know him. It knew him as the man who slew Goliath and achieved a world-wide fame; as a man whose name was a tower of strength, and whom it was a formidable thing to meet in the battle-day; as the sweet psalmist of Israel; as the king who reigned in Jerusalem. And yet it did not know him. "I am a stranger in the earth." There was that in and about him which made the earth strange to him, and which made him strange in the earth. So it is to-day. The world knows the saint in a sense, and yet it does not know him. The world knows his gentleness, his integrity, his unwearied beneficence, his patience, his love, his truth. But it does not know *himself*. The world knows systematic theology, it knows exegesis, it knows consistent profession, it knows Broad Churchism, it knows exact payments and liberal housekeeping and exemplary conduct. But it does not know *the inner life of a saint*—that secret life which is hid with Christ in God; that spark divine kindled in the soul in the day of regeneration which all the floods of corruption and temptation cannot quench, and which will shine like the sun in the Father's kingdom. "Your life is hid with Christ in God." The *author* of this inner life, the Holy Ghost; its *nature* as spiritual and Christ-like and divine: its *fruits* appearing in the graces of a holy walk and conversation, like ripe apples bending the branches to the ground; and its glorious *destiny* in heaven, are all unknown to the world. A saint, though poor as Lazarus, is an angel in disguise. A dazzling crown of glory hangs over his head. Angelic squadrons keep guard around him. The voice, "Come up hither," will soon sound in his ears from an open heaven. And this inner life of the saint introduces him into a new relation to God as his Father, to Jesus as his elder Brother, to the Church of the first-born as his brethren, and to heaven as his home, which is all a mystery to the world. The joys and sorrows of this inner life, its hopes and fears, its struggles and victories, its privileges and prospects, are all unknown to the world. How "a stranger in the earth" is effectually called, and adopted into the family of God, and justified, and sanctified—how the King's daughter is all glorious within, although her outward condition is so mean and despised—the world cannot understand. "I am a stranger in the earth." "The world knoweth us not."

3. *The saint's portion is not upon the earth.*

A stranger generally has no house nor home, no friends nor property, in the place where he is a stranger. His home and heart are away. So is it with him who is a stranger in the earth. His portion is not here. His home and treasure and heart are above. He desires a better country, that is, an heavenly.

I have heard of the owner of a princely

mansion and vast estates who was a distinguished Christian. He had his stud and his park—his gilded carriages and his servants in rich liveries. But—rare miracle of divine grace—he was more remarkable for his meek and humble piety than for his wealth. One day a Christian brother, in humble life, called at the great house to see him. The poor man felt ill at ease amid such grandeur, and looking round on the splendid scene before him, exclaimed, "This is a very fine place, sir." "Yes," said the owner, meekly, "but it's yours as well as mine!" Ah! he had a better portion above—he had a more splendid property in the bright plains of heaven—

> "On the other side of Jordan,
> In the sweet fields of Eden,
> Where the tree of life is blooming."

So it was with David. He had a kingdom and a palace-royal on earth; but these were not his portion. He was entirely weaned from them. "I am a stranger in the earth." "Thou art my portion, O Lord. The Lord is the portion of mine inheritance and of my cup.

Whom have I in heaven but thee, and there is none upon earth that I desire besides thee."

And so is it with every child of God. His inheritance is above. He is born heir to it, and has a title to it. The Bible is the charter; it contains the title-deeds of his inheritance. For every heir to an estate must show papers, documents, title-deeds—perhaps he can show a royal charter as old as Alfred, or Robert Bruce. And as the heir feels a pleasure in examining the charter which secures him his estate, so the saint loves his Bible. If the Bible gives you a title to property in the heavenly Canaan, God will not dispute that title; if the Bible gives you no title, God will give you none. And the heir of heaven receives the earnest of his inheritance, as the heir to a great estate has his maintenance off the estate during his minority. And he is daily being qualified for it. "Our conversation is in heaven," said Paul. Our Father, our elder Brother, our brethren and sisters, our home, our eternal portion, our hearts are in heaven!

> "I'm but a stranger here,
>   Heaven is my home;
> Earth is a desert drear,
>   Heaven is my home.
> Danger and sorrow stand
> Round me on every hand,
> Heaven is my fatherland,
>   Heaven is my home."

We read of some "who have their portion in this life," and none beyond. "They send forth their little ones like a flock, and their children dance. They take the timbrel and harp, and rejoice at the sound of the organ. They spend their days in wealth, and in a moment go down to the grave." How awful to have one's home and heart on earth, and at death to be driven away into the dreadful dark of eternity, without a friend, without a home.

4. *The saint is compassed with sorrows and trials upon earth.*

It is a weary thing to be far from home, where you can never see the light of a father's smile, nor hear the dear mother-tongue—to sojourn among strangers who look coldly at you, or among enemies who annoy you. Strange faces, a strange language, strange houses, strange manners, strange scenes, make the heart long for home. And your money is apt to run short. So this wilderness is a weary scene to the stranger in the earth. "In the world ye shall have tribulation. Marvel not if the world hate you." The world that crucified Jesus will crucify his disciples too. Like Abraham among the Canaanites—like Lot in Sodom—like the Israelites in Egypt—like Christian and Faithful at Vanity Fair, where they were treated as the filth of the earth, and the offscouring of all things—so is the heavenward-bound stranger in the midst of a hating, persecuting world. Ask the heir of glory, and he will say, "I am not at home—I am not at rest here—I am like a ship afar at sea lashed by the tempest—like a soldier in the grim strife of the battle-field—I cannot for a moment lay the pilgrim staff aside: Oh, to be home!"

>"Had I the wings of a dove, I would fly
> Far, far away ; far, far away :
> Where not a cloud ever darkens the sky
> Far, far away ; far, far away.

> Fadeless the flowers in yon Eden that blow,
> Green, green the bowers where the still waters flow,
> Hearts, like their garments, are pure as the snow,
> Far, far away ; far, far away."

Sometimes, it is true, you come to a sweet spot in the wilderness, like Elim with its fountains and refreshing shade. Sometimes Jesus sends you clusters of Eshcol grapes—foretastes of glory. He makes a day in his courts better than a thousand. And sometimes you meet a fellow-traveller bound for Canaan like yourself, and your heart is glad. But still the stranger longs for home. He longs for his Father's house. He longs to see the King in his beauty, and the land that is very far off. He is home-sick. Blessed are the home-sick, for they shall reach home.

5. *The saint is soon to leave the earth.*

"I am a stranger in the earth." "I am a poor dying sinner. My days are short here." A stranger never stays long in a place—a day or two—he hurries from scene to scene—he inspects everything with deep interest. You see him busy consulting maps and guide-books — busy inquiring about roads and guides and means of travel, and the quickest route home—busy examining the progress he has already made—busy settling accounts and preparing for his departure: and early next morning he is away. Look at him. His great aim is to press forward on his journey. He admires the scenes through which he passes, but he would not live among these scenes: his heart is at home. His friends expect him at home. A happy welcome awaits him at home. He sees lovely landscapes—he sees the sweep of mighty forests, and roaring water-falls—he sees magnificent amphitheatres of hills, with peaks of everlasting snow—he sees spots hallowed and immortalized by genius, like the Avon or Abbotsford—he sees grand reaches of the ocean—he sees proud or classic cities with their domes and towers, and pinnacles and spires; he admires it all, and passes on. Ask him whether he admires all this. He says, Yes. Ask him whether he would not live here and put off his journey. He says, No, because his heart and thoughts are at home.

Thus the saint looks with a traveller's eye

upon the world. "I am soon to leave this beautiful world," said the venerable Dr. Duncan lately to a friend, "and I am anxious to carry as perfect a calotype of it as I can along with me; and therefore I gaze with unwearied delight upon the trees and flowers, and the blue sky and the faces of men."

II. THE SHORT APPLICATION.

"I am a stranger in the earth." 1. *Don't be like the world.* "Be not conformed to this world." Don't be like the children of the world in *dress.* "The pilgrims were clothed," says Bunyan, "with such kind of raiment as was diverse from the raiment of any that traded in Vanity Fair." Be clothed with the righteousness of Christ.

> "Jesus, thy robe of righteousness
> My beauty is, my glorious dress;
> No age can change its lovely hue,
> Its glory is forever new."

"Let thy garments be always white, and let thy head lack no ointment." Don't be like the world in *speech.* Speak the language of Canaan. Let thy speech "bewray thee." *Confess* that you are a stranger and a pilgrim in the earth. Make no secret of it. Declare plainly that you seek a country. "He that is of the earth is earthly, and speaketh of the earth.

2. Be prepared to be a *sufferer* in the earth. The only crown that the world had for your Master was a crown of *thorns*. If you are a stranger in the earth, you will be a sufferer in the earth. Think it not strange concerning the fiery trial which is to try you. They who are now clothed in white robes with palms in their hands, came out of great tribulation. "If ye were of the world, the world would love his own: but because ye are not of the world, but I have chosen you out of the world, therefore the world hateth you." And Satan walketh about like a roaring lion. You cannot expect home comforts in the wilderness. Inns are useful—but not for permanent abode. They are only intended to fit the stranger for pursuing his homeward journey the faster. You may get foretastes now—glimpses through the lattice—but not the full enjoyment. Don't be like the cross infant that frets and bawls except when

it's being nursed. How lightly Paul took his trials! "Our light affliction is but for a moment."

> "What though the tempest rage,
>   Heaven is my home :
> Short is my pilgrimage,
>   Heaven is my home ;
> And Time's wild wintry blast
> Soon will be overpast,
> I shall reach home at last,
>   Heaven is my home."

3. *Sit loose to the world.*

A stranger does not mix himself up with affairs in the place where he is a stranger. Shake yourself free of the world's entanglements and cares, its companies and pleasures. "How long have I to live?" said the good old Barzillai; "better for me to prepare for my grave." Hear M'Cheyne's solemn words, "A believer stands on a watch-tower—things present are below his feet—things eternal are before his eyes. . . . Time is short. The disease is now in the body of many of you that is to lay you in the dust; and your grave is already marked out. In a little while you will be lying quietly there. . . . Be ready to leave your loom for the golden harp: be ready to leave your desk for the throne of Jesus; your pen for the palm of victory: be ready to leave the market below for the streets of the New Jerusalem, where the redeemed shall walk. If you were in a sinking ship, you would not cling hard to bags of money—you would sit loose to all, and be ready to swim. This world is like a sinking ship, and those who grasp at its possessions will sink along with it." Again we say, *Sit loose to the world.* Don't mingle freely with it.

One of the grand sights in the neighborhood of Geneva is the junction of the Rhone and the Arve. The Rhone is blue and pure as the heavens—the Arve is foul and muddy as the clay. They fall into the same channel—they meet—without commingling. The Rhone is the type of heaven's blue purity in a regenerate soul; the Arve is the type of the world's earthliness. The Rhone runs along the north bank, and the Arve along the south. The line between the pure waters and the foul is as straight as an arrow. The pure seems to say to the foul, "Don't come near me." The separation is complete though they flow in the same channel. The separation is complete as long as the current of the Rhone is swift. By and by the current of the Rhone becomes sluggish, and the two commingle—and the Rhone's waters are now as foul and clayey as those of the Arve.

For a time after you have been washed in the Bath of regeneration, you run fast. You look for and haste unto the coming of the day of God. You say, "Why is his chariot so long a coming? why tarry the wheels of his chariots?" And though surrounded by the clayey waters of the world's companionship, you remain separate, and you preserve the blue purity—the whiteness of your soul:—you speed swiftly homewards. But if you relax your efforts and become sluggish, you will soon become foul and clayey like the world.

4. *Correspond with home.*

It is a relief to a stranger to write home—and oh, a letter from home in a strange land is sweet. One mark of a dutiful son in a strange land is, that he often writes home. What would you think of the boy away among strangers who never wrote to his father or mother? Stranger in the earth! prayer is your means of correspondence with home. The throne of grace is the spiritual post-office. The stranger in the earth cannot write home aright himself. A proof surely how weak and helpless he is—for how poor the creature who cannot even write a letter! But the Holy Spirit helps him to write. (Rom. viii. 26.) And he directs his letters to his Father under the care of his Elder Brother. He expects an answer where he posted his letter—at the footstool of Divine grace. The answer arrives in due time: and often a remittance—a fresh supply of grace—arrives to help the stranger in his distress. Men talk of telegraphs. Prayer is the quickest of all telegraphs. Gabriel is made to fly swiftly to touch and talk with the lone stranger in the earth. Oh, then, *correspond with home.* Pray without ceasing.

5. *Cherish brotherly love for your fellow-strangers in the earth.*

They tell us that no love is so tender as that which knits fellow-countrymen who meet in a foreign land. Far from their common home, they are thrown more closely together. They are exposed to the same difficulties and dangers. They have many interests in common. They have many touching associations—many sorrows and hopes—in common: and all this knits their hearts with a tie of no ordinary tenderness.

Some years ago, early on a summer morning, the writer was wandering alone through the streets of Geneva. Feeling lonely, he was thinking of home. Turning the corner of a street, he saw a fellow-townsman coming up to meet him. The face was familiar, but the two had never exchanged a word. They had passed each other innumerable times on the street at home. But meeting abroad, a common feeling of being in a strange land—a common love for the dear mother tongue—a common longing for home, knit them almost inseparably together. They felt like brothers. Oh! surely those who are washed in the same blood—who are sanctified by the same Spirit—who are fed by the same Manna—who are refreshed with water from the same Living Rock—who are guided by the same Cloudy Pillar—who are bound for the same glorious Canaan—should love each other very tenderly when they are strangers in the earth. "Love the brotherhood." Help your fellow-pilgrims. How lovingly Christian and Hopeful helped each other when walking across the Enchanted Ground!

6. *Hasten Home.* Dispatch your work here. Desire the better country, that is, the heavenly. Set your affections upon it. Have your conversation in it. Be conformed to it. Look forward to your removal to it. Like Moses from the top of Pisgah, view "the good land that is beyond Jordan, that goodly mountain and Lebanon." Like the pilgrims from the Delectable Mountains, look "through the perspective glass of faith towards the gates of the celestial city." Come up from the wilderness *daily* leaning on your Beloved. Like Samuel Rutherford, "speak much of the white stone and the new name." Prepare for going home. Let your loins be girt and your lamp burning. When you reach home you will not be a stranger

there. You will be made a pillar in the temple of God, and go no more out. *Heaven is in full bloom.* The many mansions are all ready. The crowns of glory, the dazzling robes, the eternal palms, the well-tuned harps are ready. Heaven's crystal doors are open to admit the weary stranger. Angels are waiting to receive the commission to bear you home. And your Father and your Elder Brother are waiting.

> "Beautiful heaven, where all is light;
> Beautiful angels, clothed in white;
> Beautiful harps through all the choir;
> Beautiful strains that never tire;—
> There shall I join the chorus sweet,
> Worshipping at the Saviour's feet!"

7. Dear strangers in the earth! *press others to come with you.* Emigrants are loud in praising their adopted country. They press others to come with them. Go and do likewise. Especially now that you have been under the chastening rod, say to them, "Come with us, and we will do you good." On every hand you see children and young men and maidens *going down* to the wilderness to wander through its dry places in search of pleasure, and to die.

Their steps are light, and their hearts are merry. This deceitful world seems a smiling paradise—a perfect Eldorado—in their eyes. They don't see the serpent's fang. They don't fear the lost eternity. Oh! say to them, with a true missionary's love, "Arise and depart, for this is not your rest: because it is polluted." "I know that my Redeemer liveth." "Our light affliction, which is but for a moment, worketh for us a far more exceeding and eternal weight of glory." "Then shall the righteous shine forth as the sun in the kingdom of their Father."

> "There is a land of pure delight,
>   Where saints immortal reign;
> Infinite day excludes the night,
>   And pleasures banish pain.
>
> "There everlasting spring abides,
>   And never-with'ring flowers:
> Death, like a narrow stream, divides
>   That happy land from ours.
>
> "Sweet fields beyond the swelling flood
>   Stand dressed in living green,
> So to the Jews old Canaan stood,
>   While Jordan rolled between.
>
> "Could we but climb where Moses stood,
>   And view the landscape o'er,
> Not Jordan's streams, nor death's cold flood,
>   Should fright us from the shore."

VII.

THE FRIENDSHIP OF THE SAVIOUR AND THE SAVED.

John xv. 15.

"Henceforth I call you not servants; for the servant knoweth not what his lord doeth: but I have called you friends; for all things that I have heard of my Father I have made known unto you."

SINCE the day when the soul of Jonathan was knit with the soul of David, so that they loved each other as their own souls, *friend* has been a sacred name. One of loving heart, loving thoughts, loving words, loving deeds. In this vale of tears a true friend is a blessed solace. Poets have sung the praises of friendship, and named it "the cement of the soul, the sweetener of life, and solder of society." Philosophers have sounded its praises. The great Lord Bacon has said that it redoubles our joys and cuts our griefs in half. When all is well with us, a friend is a mighty help; when all is dark, he is a blessed beam of light. There is hardly a subject to which such continual reference is made in the literature of every land, on which so many books have been written, so many eulogiums pronounced in prose and verse. It touches every heart. The dullest can understand that life is a dismal solitude without a friend.

The text reveals Jesus in the character of a friend. He has been exhorting his disciples to love one another, and he adds this consideration to give weight to the exhortation. (Vers. 12–15.) I have called you *friends*. We are knit together in the bonds of a very close relationship. You are friends; I am your friend. I have admitted you to free and unrestrained fellowship. I have unbosomed myself to you. I am going to give you the most amazing of all proofs of my friendship—to lay down my life for you. Be this your great example. Love one another as I have loved you.

Some have understood the word " Henceforth " as indicating different stages in the teaching of Jesus, as if at one stage he had called them servants and at another friends. It rather distinguishes between the disciples' place under his personal teaching, and their place under the teaching of the Spirit after his ascension, when the whole scheme of truth was unveiled. The word servant is used in two senses, a lower and a higher. In its higher sense the relation of servant and that of friend were to subsist together. (Ver. 20.) The servant relation was not to be abolished but glorified: and there is no name by which the disciple better loves to call Jesus than " My Master."

> "How sweetly doth *my Master* sound! *my Master!*
> As ambergris leaves a rich scent unto the taster,
> So do these words a sweet content,
> An oriental fragrancy, *my Master*."—HERBERT, 223.

But now, under the dispensation of the Spirit, the special name he gives his disciples is friends. "I have called you friends." The saint is never without a friend. He may have but a humble dwelling—he may be poor, despised, companionless: but you cannot pass by his door and say, "There lives a friendless man." No! he has a Friend that sticketh closer than a brother, —a Friend more reliable and helpful than all earthly friends,—a Friend who can show himself friendly when human help and sympathy are of no avail.

The elements of true friendship are *love, confidence, sympathy,* and *help:* and as friendship has two sides, our subject branches into two divisions.

I. CHRIST'S SIDE OF THE FRIENDSHIP.

This includes—1. Christ's *love to us.* Love is the soul of friendship. The outward manifestations of friendship—the kind words and looks—the letters expressing the inmost feelings of the heart—the gifts—all derive their value from the love which is its soul. Think of that love which is the soul of Christ's friendship. He puts forward only one side of it in the context—that it made him lay down his life for his friends. To die for a friend is the very highest proof of human love. The friendship of Damon and Pythias in classic story is immortalized by their willingness to die for each other. When Damon was condemned to die, he got leave from the tyrant to go home to settle his affairs on condition that he would return for execution. Pythias offered to suffer for him if he did not return in time. Damon returned at the hour appointed, and the tyrant was so amazed at their mutual self-sacrifice that he liberated both. But the love of Christ surpassed this highest manifestation of human love. He died for his enemies, in order to make them friends. (Rom. v. 8.) His love had no beginning. It glowed in his heart before the foundation of the world. It cannot be measured. "It is high as heaven, what canst thou do? deeper than hell, what canst thou know? The measure thereof is longer than the earth and broader than the sea." And when his love had to face the dreadful issue of saving his people by laying down his life, or saving his life by leaving them to perish, it made him set his face like a flint: it carried him through the Agony—the trial in the judgment-hall—the *via dolorosa*—the six hours' darkness on the cross. "I have a baptism to be baptized with, and how am I straitened till it be accomplished." "The cup that my Father hath given me, shall I not drink it?" (Luke xii. 50; John xviii. 11.)

2. Christ's *confidence*. A servant knows nothing of his master's plans and reasons. He is not admitted into confidence. He is kept at a distance. He occupies a humbler place: he sits at a humbler table. He is simply told to do his work. He receives and executes his master's orders, and he receives his wages. But a friend is very differently treated. You tell him your secret thoughts and feelings, whatever lies nearest your heart. You give him your full, unreserved confidence. He is always welcome.

So does Jesus deal with his friends. He gives them special marks of his regard. He brings them very nigh — even unto his seat — his presence-chamber. He walked with Enoch. He talked with Moses face to face, as a man talks with his friend. He took him up to the mount, and revealed to him his secret counsels, until his face shone with the light of heaven. At the courts both of David and Solomon, there was one great minister, called by way of eminence "The King's Friend," who was cognizant of all the secrets of the state. (2 Sam. xv. 37; 1 Kings iv. 5.) The King of kings admits every disciple into this relation. He is very free with them—he keeps back nothing. Abraham was called the friend of God. (2 Chron. xx. 7; James ii. 23.) How did God show his friendship towards him? By revealing his secret to him. When Sodom and Gomorrah were to be destroyed, God said, "Shall I hide from Abraham that thing which I do?" (Gen. xviii. 17.) He admitted him into his familiar confidence.

"This honor have all his saints." "They dwell in the secret place of the Most High, and abide under the shadow of the Almighty." He brings them into his chambers; they see the King's face. John leaned upon his breast at supper. He walked with the two disciples to Emmaus, he made their hearts burn within them, and opened their understandings that they might understand the Scriptures.

It is the same now. His secret is with them that fear him. To those who live near to him, he not only reveals his mind in the Word, but their interest in the blessed world to come. He tells them that they are heirs of God, and joint-heirs with Christ. His Spirit within them says in blessed whispers, "I am thine: thou art mine." And the more closely they walk with him, the more does he tell them of his mind, the greater insight he gives them into the deep things of God.

3. His *sympathy*. This is one of the natural outflowings of friendship. Those who are knit together in the bonds of friendship make the sorrows of each other their own. It is when sorrow comes that I know who *are* my friends. If one member suffers, all the members suffer with it. Thus our Glorious Head suffers in the least member of his mystical body. "He was made in all things like unto his brethren." He has all the feelings and affections of man. Hunger, thirst, weariness, want, sorrow, pain— he knew them all. He was in all points tempted like as we are, yet without sin. (Heb. ii. 18.)

We are apt to overlook his perfect humanity. We think of his Godhead, and we pray for certain spiritual blessings, such as pardon and an abundant entrance, but we forget his tender, compassionate, human heart, and his readiness to sympathize with us under the common ills of life. He is a merciful and faithful High Priest. "Can a woman forget her sucking child, that she should not have compassion on the son of her womb? Yea, they may forget, yet will I not forget thee." (Isa. xlix. 15.)

In this sin-smitten world no subject is so soothing as the sympathy of Jesus. For "sorrow is the very woof which is woven into the warp of life." Threads of sorrow enter into the experience of every day. Sickness, bereavement, pain, reproach, poverty, visit us by turns, until almost every nerve has thrilled with pain, and every affection has been wounded. Perhaps you have received the heartshock from which you will not recover in this world; and under a sense of the coldness of human sympathy, who has not said, " O for a friend who could perfectly sympathize with me, heart to heart, and pulse to pulse, could make my sorrow his own!"

Jesus is such a friend. He can enter into all your feelings. "I know their sorrows." (Exod. iii. 7.) He had compassion on the multitude because they fainted. He tenderly sympathized with the sorrowing mother at Nain, and said, "Weep not." He wept with the two sisters over the grave of Lazarus. "Jesus wept" is the true balm for the sorrow-stricken heart. And even when he went forth bearing his cross, seeing the daughters of Jerusalem bewailing and lamenting him, he forgot his own sorrows and turned to comfort them. (Luke xxiii. 28, 29.) Who can express the wonderfulness of his sympathy? Any kindness done to his people he regards as done to himself (Matt. xxv. 40); any wrong done to them as done to him— "Saul, Saul, why persecutest thou me?" (Isa. lxiii. 9; Zech. ii. 9.) He is beside you night and day. He counts your sighs and your smiles. In health he is near to guide you; in sickness, to pillow your aching head. Those sublime words, spoken to Olivet, as the up-drawing heavens opened to receive their reascending Lord, have lost none of their power after the lapse of eighteen centuries, "Lo, I am with you alway, even to the end of the world!"

4. His *help*. A friend helps a friend. Jesus not only sustains by his sympathy, but by his all-sufficient help. His arm is as strong to help as his heart is tender to feel. (Ps. xlvi. 1.) You are well assured of the sympathy of him who uttered this farewell discourse: every word is brimful of love. You may be equally assured of his power to help. "All power is given unto me in heaven and in earth." "Is there anything too hard for the Lord?" Hence we are invited to "come boldly to the throne of grace, that we may obtain mercy, and find grace to help in time of need." (Heb. iv. 16.) "A friend in need is a friend indeed." Very significant is the Greek word for to help. It means,* A *cry*—*Run*—that is, to run up at a cry—to "Haste to the Rescue:" suggesting that Jesus, the moment he hears the cry of distress, hastens from his high throne in heaven to give effectual

* βοη-θεω.

succor. The word "succor," too, conveys the same idea—to *run up to one's side*. (Ps. l. 15.) The arm that guides the sun in heaven is pledged to help you. He will help you against your *sins*. (1 John i. 7.) He will help you in the hour of temptation. "Simon, Simon, behold, Satan hath desired to have you, that he may sift you as wheat: but I have prayed for thee, that thy faith fail not." (Luke xxii. 31, 32.) He will help you when you walk in *darkness* (Mal. iv. 2); he will help you in *sorrow* (John xvi. 22); he will help you in the hour of *death* (Isa. xliii. 2); and when he has helped you over all the rough miles of the earthly pilgrimage, he will welcome you to the mansions on high. And this Friend, so loving, so confiding, so sympathizing, so helpful, is always near you, always at your side, always within call, always thinking of you, always making everything work together for your good.

II. OUR SIDE OF THE FRIENDSHIP.

"I have called you friends." Our friendship is mutual. I am your friend, you are my friend.

Brethren, if we have a friend in heaven, let us show that *he* has friends on earth. If we have a great Elder Brother on high, let us show that he has younger brethren on earth—weak, needy, helpless, but still children of the same family.

1. Christ's friends *love him in return*. They love him with a bridal love. They give him the throne of their hearts. He is the Sun in their soul's firmament. They love him above the dearest on earth. He is to them the Rose of Sharon—the bundle of myrrh in the bosom—the cluster of camphire in the vineyards of Engedi. (Ps. lxxiii. 25; Song viii. 6, 7.) A martyr of the early Church was wont to say, "My love was crucified."

This love will manifest itself by loving, adoring thoughts of him. You will be always thinking of him. Naturally, as the flame mounts upwards, where love glows like an altar-fire in the heart, it will ascend in sweet thoughts to where he is.

It will manifest itself by keeping his commandments. A holy life is the surest proof of your friendship to Christ. The love of Christ is not a mere warm sentimental emotion, but a mighty principle of action that sets every faculty in the man to work. Hence the secret of Paul's consuming labors was, "The love of Christ constraineth us."

2. They *confide in him*, they *trust him* in return. They admit him into the fullest confidence. They tell him all their secrets. I may distrust a stranger—to a friend I give all my confidence. They tell him what they would not tell father or mother—their secret thoughts. They lay them open to his eye. They lay upon him the burden of all their sins. "I lay my sins on Jesus." They ask his help against the sin which doth most easily beset them. They ask his counsel in everything. They lay open their wants to receive his ocean fulness.

> "With him sweet converse I maintain :
> Great as he is, I dare be free :
> I tell him all my grief and pain,
> And he reveals his love to me."

They embrace every opportunity of *meeting* him. Separation from him is painful. It is this that makes the closet so dear. There they have secret communings with him which it is not possible for man to utter. "His left hand is under my head," said the spouse, "and his right hand doth embrace me." *There* they take their first walk with their Friend—they sing their first song to him—they take their first meal with him—they have their first transaction with him. They commit everything to his care. They have learned that sweet word of Peter's, "Casting all your care upon him, for he careth for you." They have learned to say, in the words of a very saintly man, lately fallen asleep in Jesus, "I desire to commit all I have to thee—my friends, my family, my wealth, my business, my esteem in the world. I am willing to receive what thou givest, to want what thou withholdest, to relinquish what thou takest, to suffer what thou inflictest, to be what thou requirest, and to do what thou commandest."

3. They *sympathize* with him.

They sympathize with *the aims* of his life. He came to reveal the Father, to publish to the world that God is love, to save the lost, to destroy the works of the devil. With their whole heart and soul the friends of Christ enter into these aims : with their whole heart and soul they adopt his resolve, " My meat is to do the will of him that sent me, and to finish his work.

Again, they sympathize with his suffering members. Christ suffers in his weak members —his friends suffer with him. To visit Christ's poor—to visit the fatherless and the widow in their affliction, is a sure way of showing your friendship to him. " Who is weak and I am not weak? Who is offended and I burn not?" Look at yon couch of pain, where one of Christ's members is suffering patiently, shut out from ordinances, and thinking with meek tears of Communion Sabbaths long gone by ; if you visit him, if you pray with him, if you relieve him, if you make his sorrow your own ; by that act you are befriending the Great Friend in heaven. When Paul was lying in prison for the last time at Rome, with the four walls of a narrow dungeon around him and a bloody death before him, Onesiphorus threaded his way through the crowded metropolis, and at the risk of shame sought him out very diligently until he found him in the condemned cell. He visited him often, and his visits were very refreshing. *There* was friendship for Christ; and Paul prays that, in that great day when the whole universe shall be assembled, Onesiphorus may taste the sweetness of a Saviour's mercy!

4. They *help Christ* in return. "Is there yet any that is left of the house of Saul," said David, "that I may show him kindness for Jonathan's sake?" This was the fruit of his friendship for Jonathan. And as Jonathan took Mephibosheth to the royal table, so your friendship for Jesus will take expression in some way. The Bridegroom is away, but his Bride is still on earth, and you can help her. When Christ's cause is low, whether in a destitute lane at home, or at a foreign mission station, help it—give liberally of your money. When his name is dishonored, and his followers ridiculed, confess him boldly, and say, with no uncertain sound, "I am not ashamed of the gospel of Christ, for it is the power of God unto salvation to every one that believeth, to the

Jew first, and also to the Greek. When his Word is dishonored by the scoffer, the sceptic, the rationalist, stand up for it as the foundation of all your hopes. When his day is encroached upon, stand up for its entire sanctification, and avow that the Sabbath is the palladium of our Scottish Christianity.

I close with two words of application.

1. To the *friends of Jesus* let me say what a friend is yours! How ennobling his friendship! What a spring of everlasting consolation! It was a joy to Joseph's brethren that he was lord over all the land of Egypt; but you have a joy unspeakably greater, your dearest Friend is at the right hand of God. This Friend never changes. You have had to mourn over the fickleness of earthly friendships, and one of the saddest thoughts in the history of the world is the estrangements that often arise between friends who once were dear. In this world, a word may cost you your friend. But he never changes. (Heb. xiii. 8.) He never fails. (Heb. xiii. 5.) He never dies.

> "Friend after friend departs:
> Who hath not lost a friend?
> There is no union here of hearts
> That finds not here an end.
> Were this frail world our only rest,
> Living or dying none were blest."

But death only admits you into his immediate presence.

2. If you are not a friend of Jesus, you are poor indeed. Alas! for those whose friendships all perish at death. "If any man love not the Lord Jesus Christ, let him be Anathema Maranatha." Remember well. He offers his friendship to the unsaved. You have long rejected him; still he offers to be your friend. And nothing is so provoking as the rejection of offered friendship. If you refuse when the Heavenly Friend invites you to his house, when he offers you his friendship, his fellowship, his grace, his counsel, his tender pity, do not wonder at the words of doom which will burst in thunder from the fiery-wheeled throne, "Depart, I never knew you."

VIII.

CLOSER THAN A BROTHER.

Prov. xviii. 24.
"There is a friend that sticketh closer than a brother."

FRIENDSHIP is sweet; but brotherhood is sweeter. "A brother is born for adversity." You can trust him; you can pour your grief into his ear; the sympathetic throb of his heart is the most reviving cordial in the day of distress. Your trial is not half so sore, nor your burden half so heavy, when your brother, standing by your side, helps to bear it. Your tears are almost exchanged for smiles, when your brother mingles his tears with yours. Tenderer than the friendship which blesses the world is the tie that links brother to brother. How near must the friend be that sticketh closer than a brother! We shall speak of him for a little in this chapter. To those especially who have no brother and few friends, our words may be welcome.

This Friend sticketh closer than a brother:

1. In *relation*. The relation of brother to brother is near; the relation of Christ to a Christian is nearer. Like branches, starting from the same stem, and fed by the same sap, which grow together and intertwine: thus do brothers grow;—the same life-blood in both. But this is only *one* of a thousand emblems which illustrate the close relation of the saint to the Saviour. This relation includes all the nearest relationships of earth put together. On one occasion, as Jesus preached to the multitude, when it was sought to press upon his notice the relationship of the virgin-mother and her sons to him, he set it aside, and, stretching forth his hand towards his disciples, he said, "Behold my mother and my brethren! For whosoever shall do the will of my Father which is in heaven, the same is my brother and sister and mother." He is the Husband of the Church. In the day of regen-

eration a marriage union is formed. "My Beloved is mine, and I am his." The bond is double. He holds the saved by his Spirit: they hold him by faith. So intimate is this relation that they are "members of his body, of his flesh, and of his bones." Look at the vine and its branches. Who can see the line where the stem ends and the branch begins? There is no such line. The two are inseparable. And the stem communicates its life to the branches, until they bend with purple clusters to the ground. Such is the Friend closer than a brother. All that is dear in the names of brother, sister, father, mother, and husband, is included in his relation to his own. Himself the true Vine, they are the branches. Himself the Head of the body, they are the members. Himself the Foundation of the temple, they are the living stones. Himself the First-born, they are the younger brothers and sisters daily growing in likeness to their elder Brother. Himself the Bridegroom, they are the Bride, who, arrayed in his righteousness and adorned with the jewels of his Spirit's grace, shall one day enter into the King's palace.

2. In *love*. There are many limits to a brother's love: there are no limits to the love of this Friend. It had no *beginning*. It *never changes*, although its manifestations may change. A brother's love is changeable. If you provoke him, he takes offence, and "is harder to be won than a strong city." Distance, suspicion, the tongue of slander sharper than a serpent's tooth, reverse of fortune, loss of character, may cool a brother's love. This love never changes. Stronger than a father's, tenderer than a mother's, no sin can weary it, no ingratitude can cool it. "The mountains shall depart, and the hills be removed: but my kindness shall not depart from thee." You may lose the sense of it, if you wrap yourself in unbelief; as you lose the sun, when a dense fog hides the landscape, and the chilly rain pours from the leaden sky. But you do not ask, Where is the sun? for you know that he moves along his heaven-high road in his chariot of light. And this love never *ends*. Even in the dark valley its everlasting arms are

underneath you. And there is *one glorious contrast* between it and earthly brother-love. Earthly friends are good while you don't trouble them. The more you tax a brother's love, the colder is it apt to become: the more you tax this love, it becomes the warmer. The less you lean on earthly friends, the likelier is their friendship to last: the more you lean on *this* Friend, the oftener you knock at his door, and press into his presence, and receive out of his fulness, the more he will reveal to you the blessedness of his love. Draw often on an earthly brother for help, and he may grow weary: draw on this Friend without ceasing, and he will supply all your wants according to his riches in glory.

3. In respect of *actual presence.* You can seldom see your brother. Your spheres are far separate. Your eldest brother, finding it hard to keep the wolf from the door at home, went to Australia: the youngest, naturally of a restless, Quixotic turn, and the proximity of the sea feeding his restlessness, went to sea: another lives a hundred miles off, and you have not seen him

for years: and your sister is married in Canada. You will never meet again here. You have a brother: but in a sense you have not. Still you need never be without a friend. The Friend that sticketh closer than a brother is ever at your side. He is better than ten brothers.

And death separates brothers on earth. I lately visited a quiet spot on the shore of a beautiful lake in the Highlands. I stood over two little mounds covered with rank grass, over which the wind blew its waves of shadow. They were the graves of my brother and sister. We had once played together, and learned to pray beside the same knee. "Ah," methought, "how little conscious is this sleeping dust of the presence of the careworn figure that stands above!" Brother! when you feel thus lone, and the world has a look of weariness, and life seems a dark enigma, "stars silent above us, graves under us silent," *take heart;* remember that you have a Friend that sticketh closer than a brother. Death may tear your brother from your side, or you from his. But Jesus sticks close at death. "At once—no flight through immensity—no pilgrimage of the spheres—for the everlasting arms are the first resting-place of the disembodied soul—it will be in the bosom of Emmanuel that the emancipated spirit will inquire, 'Where am I?' and read in the face of Jesus the answer, 'Forever with the Lord.'"*

4. In respect of *power to help*. Often, after all, what can a brother do for you? Can he remove pain or suffering? Can he heal the seams and scars of a wounded soul? Can he pluck the sting from a guilty conscience? Can he exorcise the haunting reminiscences of a polluted heart? Can he deliver from death? Can he even extricate the difficulties of life? Can he open the gate of heaven? No, no. He can do none of these for himself. But the Friend closer than a brother can do all these. He can forgive all your iniquities. He can heal all your diseases. He can redeem your life from destruction. He can crown you with loving-kindness and tender mercies. He can satisfy your mouth with good things, so that your youth is renewed like the eagle's. So that, with

* "Mount of Olives," p. 45.

his omnipresence to abide with you, and his omnipotence to guard you—with his fulness to supply you, and his love to solace you—with his wisdom to counsel you, and his compassionate heart to sympathize with you—with his promises to feed you, and the light of his face to shine upon you, to shed upon you the sense of a Divine personal recognition, and to fill you with unutterable joy—you need never complain that you are without friends, that you have nothing worth living for, and that your heart is grown old and gray before the time.

The practical uses of this are obvious:

1. *Show yourself friendly to him.* "A man that hath friends must show himself friendly." To a Friend closer than a brother show yourself friendlier than to a brother. Walk with him like Enoch. Correspond with him by prayer. Meet him in those trysting-places where he records his name. You show your love to a friend by visiting his house. Frequent *his* house. Work for him. Testify for him in a dark world. "Let your light shine before men."

2. *Stick close to him*—closer than to a brother. Friendship must not be one-sided. He has loved you with an everlasting love. Give him your spark of love in return. He has reached forth his arms to receive you. Reach forth your arms to receive him. Stick to him to the last. Be like Caleb, who followed the Lord fully—with all his heart, at all hazards, all his days.

IX.

THE FIERY TRIAL.

1 Peter iv. 12, 13.

"Beloved, think it not strange concerning the fiery trial which is to try you, as though some strange thing happened unto you: but rejoice inasmuch as ye are partakers of Christ's sufferings, that, when his glory shall be revealed, ye may be glad also with exceeding joy."

THERE is not a verse in the Bible, which represents the Christian life as an easy thing. All the figures employed to describe it are suggestive of hardship and difficulty. It is a race,—and the Christian is commanded to lay aside every weight, and the sin which most easily besets him, and to press towards the mark for the prize. It is a warfare, —and the hardships incident to a soldier's life are included in it,—the toilsome march, the night-watch, the surprise, the deadly charge, the shame of defeat, the triumph of victory. It is a voyage, for those who depart from the path are said to make shipwreck; and although beacons have been planted on the reefs and light-houses on the headlands by the Lord of the country whither we are going—although the Bible is the chart and Jesus the Pilot—yet the quicksands are so treacherous, and the Euroclydon blasts so fierce, that millions have never reached the shining shores. It is a pilgrimage,—saints in all ages have confessed that they were strangers and pilgrims in the earth,—every heaven-tending soul finds its "Progress" portrayed in Bunyan's beautiful map of the journey "from this world to that which is to come,"—and recognizes another self in the lone man who left wife and children behind, and never halted till he reached the celestial city. Here it is called a fiery trial ("the burning" is the literal rendering)—trial in the furnace or fining-pot—purification by fire. "For thou, O God, hast tried us as silver is tried." "I will bring the third part through the fire, and will refine them as silver is refined, and will try them as gold is tried." (Ps. lxvi. 10; Zech. xiii. 9.) No cross, no crown—no thorn, no throne—no trial, no triumph. We never read of a bed on which the pilgrim is to sleep, or of a coach in which he is to ride in state to heaven. There is an inseparable connection between the race and the prize—between the fight of faith and the victor's throne—between the rough voyage and the entrance into the blissful haven—between the march through the wilderness and the possession of Canaan—between the tears of earth and the songs of heaven.

"Beloved, think it not strange concerning the fiery trial." Look at the tenderness of the words! This is the language of a companion in tribulation. How changed is Peter since we saw him last! He was then soldier-like, frank, impulsive, outspoken: a true disciple, no doubt, but so rash and self-confident, that he was continually starting aside. He is now calm, subdued, tender, watchful. The light of his epistles is soft as the light of the evening sun. The change is due to his grievous fall and gracious recovery. A tradition, current in the early Church, informs us, that as long as he lived he never heard the cock crow without weeping. The broken bone, when it knits and is healed, is strongest at the point of fracture. "God can make use of poison to expel poison." Strange mystery—that he can take even your sin and make it work for your soul's sanctification. "He can make the deeper sin produce the deeper penitence—he can let you down into such an abyss of self-loathing that you will rise the stronger from your very fall. As the tree is fertilized by its own broken branches and fallen leaves, and grows by its own decay;" thus by Peter's fall was his soul chastened, purified, and ripened for glory. "The Lord turned and looked upon Peter; . . . and Peter went out and wept bitterly." That great burst of love and sorrow is the secret of the tender affectionateness of the words—"Beloved, think it not strange concerning the fiery trial which is to try you."

Let us select four elements in the fiery trial, and dwell on them for a little: the *persecution of the world*—the *crucifixion of the flesh*—the *conflict with Satan*—the *crooks in the lot.*

1. The *persecution of the world.* Cain killed Abel—and Cain will kill Abel to the end of the world. The spirit of Christ and the spirit of the world are diametrically opposite. The enmity which God put between the serpent and the woman, and between the serpent's seed and her seed, rages at this hour. It may not always break forth—the venom sleeps in the folded snake—but it is there. As Ishmael persecuted Isaac, and Esau Jacob, and Saul David—so the world has persecuted the Church in all ages. See how it fared with the prophets. "Which of the prophets," said Stephen, "have your fathers not persecuted? And they have slain them which showed before of the coming of the Just One, of whom ye have now been the betrayers and murderers. (Acts vii. 52.) "And others had trial of cruel mockings and scourgings, yea, moreover, of bonds and imprisonment: they were stoned, they were sawn asunder, were tempted, were slain with the sword: they wandered about

in sheep-skins and goat-skins; being destitute, afflicted, tormented: (of whom the world was not worthy:) they wandered in deserts, and in mountains, and in dens and caves of the earth." (Heb. xi. 36–38.) Dr. John Brown is of opinion that this refers to the Maccabean martyrs. But the sufferings of the prophets, apostles, and early Christian martyrs might be described in the same words. During the first three hundred years of our era the Church was in a state of chronic persecution. You have read of the ten general persecutions during these ages of fiery trial. So fierce was the persecutors' rage that the words "To the lions with the Christians—to the lions with the atheists"—passed into a proverb. You have read the harrowing records of the sufferings inflicted upon the saints by Nero: "They were crucified. They were sewed in sacks made of the skins of wild beasts, and thrown to be torn by dogs. They were smeared with pitch, fixed upon the sharp points of poles and set on fire as torches to illuminate the imperial gardens by night." "The most illustrious victim of the martyr times was Polycarp, Bishop of Smyrna, a disciple of the apostle John. He was carried before the proconsul, and called on to curse Christ, and thus obtain his liberty. 'Eighty and six years,' he replied, 'have I served him, and he never did me any wrong; how then can I blaspheme my King and my Saviour?' He died, praising God amidst the flames, for having deemed him worthy to be numbered among his martyrs." Nothing can be more spirit-stirring than the manifestation of the power of Divine grace in these martyr times—how it made the noble sufferers insensible to the rack and the fire. Look at the fiery trials of the Reformation period. On St. Bartholomew's day, August 24, 1572, thirty thousand Protestants were butchered in Paris under the direction of Catherine de Medici; and Rome offered solemn thanksgivings to God. The bloody Mary tried to burn out the Protestant faith with the fires of Smithfield, and martyrs like Saunders, and Ridley, and Hooper, went up in the fiery chariot.

And there was a Bartholomew Day in England too. In 1662, two years after the Restoration, by what was called the act of Uniformity, more than two thousand ministers, men such as Owen and Philip Henry, Baxter and Howe, Bunyan and Joseph Alleine, were driven from their pulpits and cast upon the providence of God, because they could not conform to the Articles of the Church of England. It was then that Baxter wrote the touching lines :

> "Must I be driven from my books?
> From house, and goods, and dearest friends?
> One of thy sweet and gracious looks,
> For more than this will make amends.
>
> "My Lord hath taught me how to want
> A place wherein to put my head :
> While he is mine, I'll be content,
> To beg or lack my daily bread.
>
> "Heaven is my roof, earth is my floor,
> Thy love can keep me dry and warm :
> Christ and thy bounty are my store :
> Thy angels guard me from all harm.
>
> "As for my friends, they are not lost ;
> The several vessels of thy fleet,
> Though parted now, by tempest-tossed,
> Shall safely in the haven meet."

Need I remind you of the fiery trials of the covenanters? The year after the Act of Uniformity was passed in England, four hundred ministers in Scotland were driven from their churches for refusing to own the king's authority within the house of God. Their flocks were scattered, banished, shot down on the moor, executed on the scaffold. The sword of persecution shed the blood of eighteen thousand martyrs. These times —when Hugh M'Kail and Donald Cargill were hanged in the Grassmarket for no crime but their faithful witness-bearing for Christ, —when Alexander Peden, the Covenanter-prophet, pined in the dungeons of the Bass —when men like John Brown of Priesthill were shot like partridges by the dragoons of Claverhouse—are still remembered with a shudder as the *killing-times* of Scotland.

Blessed be God, Christ's witnesses are not now exposed to this form of fiery trial. " The fires of Smithfield are extinct, the Grassmarket gallows is taken down." All religions are tolerated now. But the spirit of the world is as much opposed to the spirit of Christ as ever. No doubt it treats religion with respect—it regards the Church as a venerable institution—it subscribes the Articles and takes the Sacrament. But if you make religion the one thing needful —if you refuse all doubtful compromises—the world will call you a fool, and then begins the fiery trial. If a son or daughter in a family is awakened, what a clamor arises! "Oh, my son or daughter is turned Methodist: she does nothing but attend meetings, and read Ryle's tracts and Spurgeon's sermons: and he is actually thinking of leaving the office and studying for the Church!" It is the fulfilment of the Saviour's words: "A man's foes shall be they of his own household." When the "Dairyman's Daughter" was converted, her sister laughed and said that her head was turned with her new ways. Is there no persecution, think you, but that of the rack and the fire? It is by scoffs and sneers, and the cold laugh of derision that the world persecutes now. "There are Sabbath-honorers who lose their employment or their trade, and keepers of a conscience who forfeit patronage and profit. And not unfrequently, I fear, is the praying youth interrupted in his devotion by scoffing room-mates, just as the Bible-reading servant or church-going artisan is made a butt and a byword by rude and jeering comrades."* Do you not persecute a man, if you shun his society and slander his good name? In our day the world's smiles are more dangerous than its frowns. They often prove a fiery trial.

2. The *crucifixion of the flesh*.

There is an old man and a new, an Adam and a Christ, in every believer. He has a double life. The old man is the saint as far as he is unrenewed, the new man is the saint as far as he is renewed. The flesh lusteth against the spirit, and the spirit against the flesh. Sin receives its death-blow, it is true, in the day of regeneration. The regenerate are baptized into Christ's death. As he was raised up from the dead by the glory of the Father, they also walk in newness of life. They are planted together in the likeness of his death, and therefore they

* "Morning Beside the Lake of Galilee," p. 90.

are planted together in the likeness of his resurrection. Their old man is crucified with him, that the body of sin might be destroyed. They are dead with Christ, and they also live with him. They enter into his resurrection life. Sin shall not have dominion over them, for they are not under the law, but under grace. They drink of the twin fountains of *peace* and *holiness* that gush forth from the cross. Their sins are all blotted out in the blood of the Lamb. Their sentence of death is cancelled, and their prison doors thrown open. Satan has now no power over them, as the executioner has no power over the man whom his sovereign has pardoned. And, finally, they receive a perfect righteousness —a righteousness so perfect that it is an unfailing passport to heaven, and, arrayed in it, they can stand unchallenged before the throne.

Then "the dynamics of sanctification"* come into play. The new life within, that came from heaven and returns to heaven—the vital union with Christ in his death and resurrection—the indwelling of the Holy Ghost, and the continual

---

* Dr. John Duncan.

supplies of his grace—the removal of the curse—the sweet sense of pardon—the operation of those mighty motives of love and adoring thankfulness to the kinsman Redeemer—these are the divine forces that will eventually destroy the body of sin. Christ made an end of sin. He bore its curse, and destroyed its power. Our old man is crucified with him. Crucifixion is death. The crucified may struggle, but he cannot come down from the cross till he dies.

The crucifixion of the flesh is a fiery trial. Crucifixion was a *painful* and a *lingering* death. So is the crucifixion of the flesh.

Painful. The old man is nailed to the cross. The death of Christ is a type of the Christian's life. As he was nailed to the accursed tree, so must our old man be. The right hand must be cut off. The right eye must be plucked out. And these words of Christ are something very much deeper and more awful than poetical symbols and metaphors. Our old, proud, corrupt self—what was our *whole* self until the day of our quickening together with Christ—must be torn with the nails, must be pierced with the spear, must drink the cup of gall. The new man must slay the old. "No holiness is won by any other means than this, that sin should be *slain* day by day, and hour by hour. In long lingering agony often, with the blood of the heart pouring out at every quivering vein, you are to cut right through the life and being of that sinful self." * Think of the pain of this! "What will ye see in the Shulamite? as the company of two armies." As if two souls struggled in one body—as if an angel of light and an angel of darkness warred within you for the mastery. The bitter spring, deep down in your soul, has been healed by casting into it the cross of Christ; but there still remains a tinge of bitterness in the sweetened waters. Brother! you must be perfected through suffering. Look at David. Turn over the Psalter, and see to how many strains the harp strings are struck. His new nature—his true self—finds expression in heavenly strains like these: "As for me, I will behold thy face in righteousness: I shall

---

* Maclaren's Sermons, p. 88. Ralph Erskine's Sermon on Gal. ii. 19. Owen on Indwelling Sin.

be satisfied when I awake with thy likeness;" "One thing have I desired of the Lord;" "My soul followeth hard after thee;" "My meditation of him shall be sweet;" "How precious also are thy thoughts unto me, O God! how great is the sum of them!" "Let everything that hath breath praise the Lord: praise ye the Lord:" but, side by side with this, his old nature, "the flesh," "the old Adam," wrings from him the sorrowful plaints: "I am weary with my groaning; all the night make I my bed to swim: I water my couch with my tears;" "My wounds stink, and are corrupt, because of my foolishness; I am troubled, I am bowed down greatly, I go mourning all the day long." As the one or the other prevails, it is joy, or tears among the willows. Look at Paul. The throb of the thorn in the flesh was sharper than "stripes," "prisons," "perils of waters," "perils of robbers," "weariness," "cold and nakedness." The sword of Nero never made him quail; it was "a light affliction which is but for a moment"—it only cut the tie that bound him to earth, and let his ransomed spirit soar on high:—the thorn in the flesh wrung from his heart a cry of agony. The crucifixion of the flesh—the putting off of the old man—is painful work. Very easy it is to say that sin, though a strong, is a wounded and dying enemy: but it is with a sore pang that the saint, who has for twenty years struggled against it, confesses with bursting tears: "I find then a law that when I would do good, evil is present with me. For I delight in the law of God after the inward man: but I see another law in my members, warring against the law of my mind, and bringing me into captivity to the law of sin which is in my members. O wretched man that I am! who shall deliver me from the body of this death?"

Lingering. The crucified often hung on the cross for hours—in some instances for days—alive. Emblem of the slow death which sin dies. Sin must die many deaths. You take part with the Spirit against it. You put it where God put it when he condemned it in the flesh. You hold it nailed to the Cross. You reckon yourself to be dead unto it, but alive unto God through Jesus Christ our Lord. You mortify, deny, resist, starve it. Still it lives and struggles. It pollutes and poisons. "In our purest moods, when we kneel to pray, or gather round the table, down into the very Holy of Holies sweep foul birds of the air, villain fancies, demon thoughts."* An old Roman tyrant had a punishment in which he bound the dead body of the murdered to the living body of the murderer. Similar is the agony of a heaven-born soul from the presence of sin. It is nailed to the Cross—Christ on the Cross cancelled our death warrant, and procured *sin's death warrant*—that blessed Cross *will* slay the fearful hydra; but it lives—it is not dead. Sometimes it gathers itself up for a desperate effort. You fall, and all seems lost. You say, "I shall now perish one day by the hand of Saul." Oh, it is a weary conflict. "Here is an enemy," says Dr. Owen, "that is never from home—an enemy whose secret windings you can only track as you

* Robertson's Sermons, i. 24.

track the underearth operations of a mole by watching the heaving surface." Imagine an inmate secretly lurking in your house who, if you turn your back, will at any moment set the house on fire. Such an inmate is sin. It lurks in dark recesses where you cannot reach it, and seeks every moment to set your soul on fire of hell. How weary is disease; and how glad is the pale invalid who has long pined in the sick-room to walk forth again, and breathe the crisp air, and see the green hills, and the sun. With such sense of weariness under the disease of sin does the believer pant for heaven. Nothing makes the thought of heaven so sweet as that there we shall sin no more. "For we that are in this tabernacle do groan, being burdened: not for that we would be unclothed, but clothed upon, that mortality might be swallowed up of life." The leprous house had to be pulled down before the leprosy could be quite rooted out of it; so this body of sin must moulder in dust ere it can be perfectly freed from the leprosy of sin.

3. The *conflict with Satan* is a fiery trial. He gives you no rest with his fiery darts. "He walketh about as a roaring lion, seeking whom he may devour." "We wrestle not against flesh and blood, but against principalities, against powers, against the rulers of the darkness of this world, against spiritual wickedness in high places."

Perhaps the most memorable passage in Bunyan's allegory is the fight with Apollyon. Apollyon means Destroyer. The battle is before and behind. You have foes without in league with foes within. Within, "the old man"—corruption six thousand years old: without, Satan in great wrath. And, like every skilful general, Satan will strive hard to hold the key of his position in your soul. The key of his position is your besetting sin. The storm of battle rages around *that*. Satan will fight there to the last. A town could easily be taken but for the batteries behind which the enemy are entrenched, and from which they pour their deadly fire; so could you easily conquer Mansoul for Prince Emmanuel but for these lusts in which the enemy is entrenched. There are two ways in which an enemy attacks —by stealth or in open fight. Satan attacks in these two: and he has two names corresponding to his two methods of attack—the serpent and the roaring lion.

(1.) As the serpent, he attacks by *stealth*. The serpent's cunning emblematizes his cunning but faintly. He deceives the whole world. And so strong is he, that when he fell he drew after him perhaps a third part of the stars of heaven —so strong that Adam, in the glory of his original righteousness, fell before him in the first encounter. As when an enemy hiding in ambush, or under cloud of night, makes the deadly sortie: so does Satan watch his opportunity. He has great experience. He knows your weak side. "He desires to have you that he may sift you as wheat." Well he knows the gate by which easiest access is got to your soul.* He keeps no Sabbath. His movements are swift as the wings of the morning. He watches

---

* "ἔνθα μαλιστα
Ἄμβατος ἐστι πολις, και ἐπιδρομον ἐπλετο τειχος."

till you are asleep, and then throws his terrible coil around you.

In the Kaffir war, the foe hid themselves in the jungle, and fired or threw the poisoned assegai at our troops. Hid in the bush we could not see them—and many a brave British life was ingloriously thrown away. "But, suppose a foe able to make themselves invisible: able to pass in a moment over leagues of country: able to live without sleep, to march without wearying, to work without food; who seldom fought but to conquer, and though repulsed often, were never destroyed: who pitied none, spared none: and regarding neither sex, nor innocence, nor age, dragged off their unhappy captives to horrible and nameless tortures—who would take the field against these? Such an enemy has no place in the pages of horrid annals of war: nor did ever man find such a foe in man. True, but he has such a foe in Satan."*

(2.) As the roaring lion, he attacks in *the open field*. The strong man armed defies the armies of the living God. How bold he is when he

* Guthrie's "Speaking to the Heart," p. 135.

tempted even the Son of God! He walketh about—he ranges the forest—seeking whom he may devour—and turneth not away from any. It is said that the lion will not eat carrion—that he disdains the putrid carcass—that he hunts for living prey. The roaring lion does not disturb those who are rotting in sin—he hunts for living souls. This is the melancholy explanation of the fact that some are not troubled by Satan's assaults. He sees that their souls are dead—without one spark of grace, without one pulse of spiritual life. A beggar who has nothing to lose is not afraid of thieves. A poor coal smack is in no danger from pirates.

My brother! remember another thing. Satan will try to cut off your supplies. A besieging enemy cuts the pipes which supply a town with water, and intercepts the wagons which supply it with victuals. Faith is the pipe that brings living water from the Fountain — the means by which all needful grace is supplied. His fiercest assaults are directed against faith. It is a fiery trial. "He wears out the saints of the Most High." "Watch, and pray that ye enter not into temptation." No sane man will venture into a sea where sharks are swimming.

4. *Crooks in your lot.* "Who can make that straight which God hath made crooked?"

Perhaps *poverty* is your crook: and with food dear and labor scarce, you hardly know how to provide bread for your children. You must live then, as many have done before you, on the sixth chapter of Matthew. Remember that Jesus was poor, and that he can sympathize with you. There is a "wealthy place" beyond.

> "The lions young may hungry be,
> And they may lack their food:
> But they that truly seek the Lord
> Shall not lack any good."

Perhaps *broken health* is your crook. You hardly know what it is to be a day well. God wishes to wean you from the world, and to turn your eyes away from its bright sights to an enduring portion. Timothy, it would seem, was very fragile. Paul tenderly counselled him in regard to his "often infirmities:" and a stricken frame kept him more intently "looking for the blessed hope." Once I visited an old saint ripening for glory. On my asking how he did, he replied, "When I am weary in the chair, they lift me into bed; when I am weary in bed, they lift me back into the chair!"

Perhaps you *hopes are broken*, and you pains and prayers seem vain. Once you threw yourself into Christ's work with unbounded hopefulness, and when he sent showers of blessing, you felt as if it were the dawn of millennial glory. There has been a reflux, and you say' "Woe is me! for I am as when they have gathered the summer fruits, as the grape gleanings of the vintage: there is no cluster to eat: my soul desired the first ripe fruit."

Or—the sorest crook of all—you are *left alone*. Bright faces that lit up your home are laid under the sod. A wife or husband is torn from your side. You cup of affliction is full. The world seems haggard. Ah, it *is* a fiery trial. "The green grass," says Mr Arnot, with characteristic pathos, "looks not so lightsome when those whom I loved the most are laid beneath it. Light is sweet; but oh, some eyes that were wont to look upon it along with me are closed now." *

Such is the furnace in which the Great Refiner purifies his gold. Such is the process by which he polishes the living stones, and fits them for their places in the heavenly temple.

* "Roots and Fruits," p. 105.

X.

THE TRIUMPH.

1 Pet. iv. 12, 13.

"Beloved, think it not strange concerning the fiery trial which is to try you, as though some strange thing happened unto you: but rejoice, inasmuch as ye are partakers of Christ's sufferings; that, when his glory shall be revealed, ye may be glad also with exceeding joy."

IN blessed contrast to the four forms of fiery trial, four causes of triumph are stated here. 1. Trial is not a strange thing in the Christian life. 2. Trial is intended to try — to purify — the saints. 3. Saints in trial are partakers of Christ's sufferings. 4. When Christ's glory shall be revealed, the suffering saints shall be glad with exceeding joy.

1. *Trial is not a strange thing in the Christian life.*

It is not a *new* thing. God had one Son, without sin, but he never had a Son without suffering. The saints' trials began nearly six thousand years ago. Abel sealed his testimony with his blood. By it, he being dead, yet speaketh. Noah was the butt of a generation who mocked at the coming flood. He grew gray preaching repentance—and his preaching only " condemned the world." Come down to Abraham, Isaac, and Jacob. What changeful, suffering careers—Abraham's especially! Strangers and pilgrims in the earth, they found that here there is no continuing city, no "place of honorable quiet for the Emeritus, no rest for the Christian soldier except in the grave. And their trials did not become lighter as they went on. Harder and yet harder trials." Wave followed wave till they reached the happy shore. Look at Moses, whose burden was often like to wear him away—David hunted as a partridge upon the mountains—the prophets weeping between the porch and the altar! Did they not suffer trial?

And did not Christ forewarn his disciples of this: "These things have I spoken unto you, that ye should not be offended. They shall put you out of the synagogue: yea, the time cometh that whosoever killeth you will think that he doeth God service. . . . In the world ye shall have tribulation." (John xvi. 1, 2, 33.) Did not Paul teach the same lesson, that the churches might not take offence at the Cross? "We must through much tribulation enter into the kingdom of God." (Acts xiv. 22.) The badge of a disciple is the Cross. Popery has many painted and gilded crosses—its devotees love to wear them: every true disciple has a *real* cross to bear. The redeemed in glory came out of great tribulation. By a narrow, steep, thorny path, they climbed onward and upward. Brother! if you are suffering fiery trial, you are in glorious company.*

* "The march of the army of God may be tracked by their ashes left behind them. The course of the ship of glory may be traced by the white sheen of suffering left on the sea of time. Like as a meteor when it flashes in its glory leaves a blaze behind it for a moment, so hath the Church left behind it blazing fires of persecution and

"Behold what witnesses unseen
　Encompass us around;
Men, once like us, with suffering tried,
　But now with glory crowned."

And it is not *strange*. It stands to reason. If you were of the world, the world would love you. But because you are not of the world, but he has chosen you out of the world, therefore the world hates you. You are a stranger in the earth—a bird of passage on your way to the Better Land—and therefore you will be a sufferer in the earth. You are as the lily among thorns, expect scratches; you are as sheep among wolves, expect not only to hear their howls but to feel their teeth. Grace is a rare exotic, a plant heavenly fair. But it does not show its loveliest tints, nor inhale its sweetest fragrance, in our cold atmosphere. It needs the serener skies, the balmier air, the never-setting sun of paradise.

2. *Trial is sent to try—to purify—the saints.*

trouble. The path of the just is scarred on earth's breast, the monuments of the Church are the sepulchres of the martyrs. You will not find the saints of God where you do not find the furnace burning round about them."—*Spurgeon*.

There is much dross in us, and the fire of affliction is needed to purge it away. We are so constituted that suffering is necessary to purify us. Here we must walk entirely by faith. We cannot tell *how* suffering purifies. Let us be satisfied when God tells us that it *is* so. Let us believe, that because our Father has ordained it, it is ordained in infinite love and wisdom. "What I do, thou knowest not now, but thou shalt know hereafter." A child does not like to be sent to school—does not see the good of it—and would prefer to climb the hills or gather flowers by the brook: its father says, "You shall go,"—and that settles it.

Affliction is the furnace—the refining pot—in which he purifies his gold. Saints are his gold: in the furnace of affliction he makes the lustre of their graces shine with peculiar brilliance. "Behold, I have refined thee, but not with silver: I have chosen thee in the furnace of affliction." As the goldsmith sits by the fining pot, and watches the molten gold till he sees his image reflected in it: so the Great Refiner watches beside his saints in their fiery trials, until their dross is removed, and his full-formed image reflected in them. "When he hath tried me," said Job, "I shall come forth as gold." The gold loses nothing but its dross in the fire. Nebuchadnezzar's fire burned nothing but the bands that bound the three holy children, and the men that cast them in.

There is no teacher like sorrow. Other things being equal, the disciple who has been longest in the school of affliction is most Christlike. In a keen night, as the stars glance most brightly in the ebon sky; so do faith, love, lowliness, patience, shine with growing brightness in the night of weeping. "Blessed is the man whom thou chastenest and teachest him out of thy law." By affliction God darkens the room and reveals himself. Affliction teaches lessons that nothing else will teach. It reveals a Father's *love*. "Whom the Lord loveth, he chasteneth." It teaches *patience*—complete surrender to God, dropping into his hand, and lying passive there. "The trying of your faith worketh patience." It *weans* from the world. How worthless it appears when you are laid on the sick-bed, and hear the rushing of the dark river! And it burnishes all your graces. It is said of the sandal-wood tree, that every stroke the woodman gives it only draws forth a breath of sweetest fragrance. So every trial draws forth the fragrance of grace. "Old Betty was converted late in life, and though very poor, was very active. She visited the sick: out of her own poverty she gave to those who were still poorer, collected a little money from others when she could give none of her own, and told many a one of the love of the Saviour. At last she caught cold and rheumatism, and lay in bed month after month, pain-worn and helpless. A good minister went to see her, and asked if, after her active habits, she did not find the change hard to bear. 'No, sir, not at all. When I was well, I used to hear the Lord say, day by day, Betty, go here, Betty, go there; Betty, do this, Betty, do that, and I used to do it as well as I could. And now I hear him say every day, Betty, lie still and cough!'"*

* Hamilton's "Lake of Galilee," p. 91.

"The furnace," says Spurgeon, "is very useful to God's people, because *they get more light there than anywhere else.* If you travel in the neighborhood of Birmingham, or in other manufacturing districts, you will be struck at night by the glare of light which is cast by all those furnaces. It is labor's own honorable illumination. I believe there is no place where we can learn so much, and have so much light cast upon Scripture, as we do in the furnace. Read a truth in tranquillity, read it in peace, read it in prosperity, and you will not make anything of it. Be put inside the furnace (and nobody knows what a bright blaze is there who has not been there), and you will then be able to spell all hard words, and understand more than you could without it. . . . Trouble exercises our graces, and the exercise of our graces tends to make us more comfortable and happy. Where showers fall most, there the grass is greenest. I suppose the fogs and mists of Ireland make it the 'Emerald Isle:' and wherever you find great fogs of trouble, and mists of sorrow, you always find emerald-green hearts—full of the beautiful verdure of the comfort and love of God." *

3. *Saints in trial are partakers of Christ's sufferings.*

They suffer with him. They are "crucified with him." They "go forth unto him without the camp, bearing his reproach." They drink of his cup, and are baptized with his baptism. Paul earnestly desired to know "the power of his resurrection, and the fellowship of his sufferings, being made conformable unto his death."

This participation in Christ's suffering does not refer to his meritorious sufferings as an Atonement for sin. These were finished at once and forever by his sacrifice upon the cross. He bare our sins in his own body upon the tree. Our sins were piled, and crowded, and massed around that accursed tree—and he made an *end* of them. He annihilated them. He cried, "It is finished." His expiatory sufferings were incommunicable—they were his own personal burden—they were perfect. They are imputed to us—and we reap the blessed fruit. The sinless

* Spurgeon's "Gems," 305, 328.

was made sin for us, that we might be made the righteousness of God in him. JESUS ONLY is the Propitiation—the sweet-smelling sacrifice—the eternal redemption.

But as Christ suffered in his person, so does he suffer in his members. The Church is his body—his second self. She has a cup to drink—a cross to bear. As every part of his literal body suffered, so must every member of his spiritual body. As his back was torn with the scourge, his face covered with shame and spitting, his hands and feet pierced with the nails, his side with the spear;—so must all his living members suffer with him. As he went by the cross to the crown, so must we. As he was straitened until his baptism should be accomplished, so must we. We must drink into the Spirit of the Cross;—its love—its self-sacrifice. Our life must be moulded after his. The same submission to the Father's will, which said, "The cup which my Father hath given me, shall I not drink it?"—must reconcile us to our cup of hourly sorrows and trials. As he died for sin, we must die to it. As he was forever freed from sin in his death, so must we be forever freed from it by his death.

In Col. i. 24, Paul uses these remarkable words, "Who now rejoice in my sufferings for you, and fill up that which is behind (the deficiencies) of the afflictions of Christ in my flesh." The Church has her measure—her cup—of afflictions meted out to her. Paul means, "I am one with Christ. My sufferings are his sufferings. As a member of Christ, a certain share of suffering is allotted to me. I have suffered part of it already, and in the sufferings I now bear for you, I am joyfully filling up the remainder."

"Rejoice inasmuch as ye are partakers of Christ's sufferings." Count it an honor to suffer reproach, to bear scars for him. His worst things excel the world's best. Moses esteemed the reproach of Christ greater riches than the treasures of Egypt. He suffers with you. "In all their affliction he is afflicted." "When I sigh," wrote Samuel Rutherford, from his prison in Aberdeen, "Christ sighs!"

The story of Margaret M'Lauchlan and Margaret Wilson, the one an aged widow, the other a tender maiden of eighteen, will be held in everlasting remembrance. They were sentenced by Claverhouse's dragoons to be drowned in the Solway. At low tide they were fastened to stakes driven in the ooze. The aged widow was placed farthest out, that she might die first. As the waters rose to her lips, and her dying struggles began, a heartless ruffian asked Margaret Wilson, who was standing in shallower water, "What do you think of your friend now?" Calmly she answered, "I see Christ in one of his members suffering there. Think you that we are the sufferers? No, it is Christ in us—for he sends none a warfare on his own charges." She was plunged into the rising waters, and received the martyr's crown.

One day, as William Burns preached in the streets of Montreal, he was roughly handled by a popish crowd. Some of them threw stones, one of which struck the preacher's face. A party of the 93d Highlanders rushed to the rescue, and one asked in anxiety, "What's all this?" Mr. Burns quietly wiped off the blood, and said, with a smile, "Never mind; it's only a little wound received in the Master's service!" Like Peter and John, departing from the presence of the council, he rejoiced that he was counted worthy to suffer shame for the name of Jesus.

4. *When Christ's glory shall be revealed, the suffering saints shall be glad with exceeding joy.*

The victory makes the soldier forget the struggles of an arduous day. When the ship enters the harbor, the sense of safety and the welcome of joyful friends are sweeter after the fearful storm. Ah, how light will the sufferings of earth appear when you look back from the glorious plains of heaven! Do the saints on high—even those who had trial of cruel mockings and scourgings—who were stoned and sawn asunder—now grudge their utmost sacrifices? Well did Paul "reckon that the sufferings of this present time are not worthy to be compared with the glory which shall be revealed in us." "For our light affliction, which is but for a moment, worketh for us a far more exceeding and eternal weight of glory." And as effect is heightened by contrast, the remembrance of the fiery trial will heighten the blessedness of heaven. Its songs will be louder after the sorrows of earth. The sharper the cross, the brighter the crown. No doubt an elect infant, taken home without tasting the sorrows of the world, will find heaven a place of blessedness. But to the toil-worn laborer it is a *Rest*. As " the sleep of a laboring man is sweet," so sleep in Jesus is passing sweet after the burden and heat of the day. The more galling the taunts of an alien world, the gladder will be your arrival at home. The sorer the conflict with sin, the more blessed will be the eternal deliverance from it. There you will sin no more. The fiercer the fight with Satan, the more triumphant the shout of " Victory, victory, through the blood of the Lamb!" (Rev. xii. 11.) The more trying the crooks in your lot, the more perfect will be the sense of relief as you see every crook made straight, and every mystery plain, in the beatific vision of God.

Cheer up, fellow-sufferer! Hold on, hold on,

for a little. "The trial of your faith is much more precious than of gold that perisheth, though it be tried with fire, and shall be found unto praise, and honor, and glory at the appearing of Jesus Christ." "When his glory shall be revealed, ye shall be glad with exceeding joy." The first hour of heaven will make up for all! "*Exceeding* joy,"—joy without alloy—joy which eye hath not seen, nor ear heard, nor heart conceived—joy ever increasing—never-ending joy—joy which, wave on wave, will flow forever into the hearts of the ransomed.

One who has lately gone from us, and passed within the veil—an Enoch for close walking with God, a Nathanael for simplicity, a John for lovingness, a Barnabas for tenderness, an Epaphras for fervent laboring in prayer (with hand uplifted like Moses' rod), and a Boanerges for unflinching boldness in rebuking sin—John Milne of Perth—speaking of this "exceeding joy," says, "They are singing and harping with all their might. They are singing in unison, and they are singing universally. No hands without a harp, no lips without a song: and no harp is unstrung, no lips are silent there. Could you approach the gate, you would hear sweetest music. They are feasting, they are rejoicing. The work is done, the fight is over, their wanderings are ended, they are all at home. Not one is lost, not one is wanting. There never was joy like this. As they look *back*, and think what they were: look *down*, and think what, but for grace, they must have been: look *around*, and see where they are: look *forward*, and think what they shall forever be, —it is joy, joy, joy! Each kindles and stirs up the other. 'Oh, that will be joyful, joyful, joyful, when we meet to part no more.' "

"Beyond the smiling and the weeping,
Beyond the waking and the sleeping,
Beyond the sowing and the reaping,
    I shall be soon.

"Beyond the blooming and the fading,
Beyond the shining and the shading,
Beyond the hoping and the dreading,
    I shall be soon.

"Beyond the gathering and the strowing,
Beyond the ebbing and the flowing,
Beyond the coming and the going,
    I shall be soon.

> "Beyond the parting and the meeting,
> Beyond the farewell and the greeting,
> Beyond this pulse's fever-beating,
>   I shall be soon."—Dr. BONAR.

" If we suffer, we shall also reign with him." The other side is, "*If we deny him, he also will deny us.*" My dear friend, make your choice to-day. The alternatives are *fiery trial*—and exceeding joy : or *ease*—and everlasting shame ; at Christ's appearing. Do you shrink from trial? You cannot escape it in any case. "The way of transgressors is hard." Do you remember the man who denied Christ for fear of being burned at Smithfield, and was afterwards burned by his own house taking fire? If you take Christ's cross, he will help you to bear it, and when you are weary, he will carry both yourself and your cross. Perhaps you are ill at ease. Perhaps conscience often stings you as it stung Colonel Gardiner in his days of sin, when, in a brilliant assembly, seeing a dog in the room, he groaned, "I wish I were that dog!" Perhaps you are easy. But what of ease—when your days are numbered—and the sword of God hangs over your head—and you are walking on a rotten covering over the mouth of hell? "A sword, a sword is sharpened, and also furbished: it is sharpened to make a sore slaughter, it is furbished that it may glitter: should we then make mirth?" Sin at last bites like a serpent, and stings like an adder. The moments of sin expand into ages of punishment. Awake, thou that sleepest. Awake—else the glorious prize will be beyond your reach. Awake—else the day of grace will be past, and death will leave you to the vultures of remorse and despair.

XI.

THE WONDERS OF THE BIBLE.

Psalm cxix. 129.
"Thy testimonies are wonderful."

A CHART which guides the navigator through the difficulties of the northern passage is considered a precious contribution to modern science. Or, if you were setting out on a journey across a wilderness of sand where a thousand caravans had perished, and you got a sure map of the course which the few successful adventurers had taken, how highly would you prize it, and how carefully would you follow its directions!

The Bible is such a chart, such a map;—the Bible, which is not prized by many as it ought to be, nor treasured in the memory, nor practised in the life,—the Bible, which in the cottages of the poor is often allowed to lie bedusted on the shelf, and in the mansions of the rich is found, no doubt, on the drawing-room table, beautifully bound and gilt, but with clasp often unfastened, from one end of the week to the other. If life is a voyage, the Bible is the chart which describes the course,—which tells of every crosstide and storm, which plants a beacon-light on every sunk rock and quicksand. If life is a journey, the Bible is a lamp to the feet and a light to the path. And not only does this Lamp Divine point out the path, but it shows the footmarks of a cloud of witnesses who have trodden it, especially the footmarks of the Forerunner; and, along the path, it tells of many a spot, like Elim, where the pilgrim may rest and enjoy blessed foretastes of heaven.

A book is wonderful if its author is possessed of wonderful wisdom, if its subject is of everlasting importance, and if its aim is the eternal good of men. The Bible has God himself for its Author, it treats of the things which belong to our peace, and its aim is to make us wise unto salvation. How wonderful then must it be acknowledged to be! Let us look at five of its wonders:

1. Its *authority*. A human author must speak modestly, and reason on principles common to him and his readers. Every other book you may set aside if you do not agree with it. Not so with the Bible. It prefaces every statement with a "Thus saith the Lord." It comes down to us like Moses from the mount, bearing the tables of the testimony. It challenges our reverence. If we refuse its words, we do it at our peril. When we open the Bible, we must do like Elijah when he heard the still, small voice, and wrapped his face in his mantle, recognizing it to be the voice of God. We must say like the child Samuel, "Speak, Lord, for thy servant heareth." The God who could speak in thunder speaks in the Bible.

Each of the sacred writers retains his peculiar individuality; and yet God speaks by him. There is as much of Moses shining through the Pentateuch as there is of Macaulay in the *His-*

tory of England. David retains his poetic ardors, Isaiah his sublimity, Jeremiah his weeping tenderness, Ezekiel his weird grandeur, John his love, Peter his boldness, Paul his insight into the mysteries of God; and yet it is God that foretells in the prophecies, that narrates in the Gospels, that comforts in the promises, that invites in the invitations.* Hence Jesus said,

---

* "The Bible is the writing of the living God. Each letter was penned with an Almighty finger: each word in it dropped from the everlasting lips: each sentence was dictated by the Holy Spirit. Albeit that Moses was employed to write his histories with his fiery pen; God guided that pen. It may be that David touched his harp, and let sweet psalms of melody drop from his fingers; but God moved his hands over the living strings of his golden harp. Solomon sang canticles of love, and gave forth words of consummate wisdom: but God directed his lips, and made the preacher eloquent. If I follow the thundering Nahum, when his horses plough the waters: or Habakkuk, when he sees the tents of Cushan in affliction: if I read Malachi, when the earth is burning like an oven: if I turn to the smooth page of John, who tells of love: or the rugged chapters of Peter, who speaks of fire devouring God's enemies: if I turn to Jude, who launches forth anathemas upon the foes of God, everywhere I find God speaking: it is God's voice, not man's: the words are God's words: the words of the Eternal, the Invisible, the Almighty, the Jehovah of ages. This Bible is God's Bible; and when I see it, I seem to hear a voice spring-

"If they hear not Moses and the prophets, neither will they be persuaded if one rose from the dead." Although a spirit from the other world, cognizant of all that is glorious in heaven, or all that is terrible in hell, should wing his way to us, and preach the gospel with all the superhuman earnestness which his actual experience of eternity would inspire;—even this appalling visitant could add nothing to the intrinsic authority of the Bible. He might startle men; but he could add nothing to the majesty and momentousness of the simple Word of God.

2. Its *light*. The natural world was a dark chaos, until God made the sun to shine upon it: and the moral world was also a dark chaos, until God shone upon it with the light of revelation.

Conceive the state of the world without the sun. Man could not live upon it. Flowers and fruits could not grow upon it. There would be no smiling summers nor golden harvests. Perpetual night would cover it as with a funeral

ing up from it, saying: 'I am the Book of God: man, read me: I am God's writing: study my page, for I was penned by God; love me, for he is my author, and you will see him visible and manifest everywhere.' "—*Spurgeon*.

pall, and wrap it in eternal gloom! Behold an emblem of the moral world without the Bible. How deplorably should we grope like the blind for the wall! There is no doubt a rudimental theology in the natural conscience; and this great universe throughout speaks of a Creator; but *sin has entered into the world;* and neither conscience nor the works of creation can cast one ray of light upon the question, How shall man be just with God? "The world by wisdom knew not God." - The brow of Plato grew sad under the infinite vault that had a pale, icy radiance, but no sun; and the speculations of the wisest heathens are but so many floating signals of distress, to show the darkness in which they sank.

The Bible is the sun in the spiritual firmament. Its light is like the light of the sun. It comes from heaven. It is warm and life-giving. It is never exhausted. There is only one sun; and there is only one Bible. A candle is a good thing, but a million candles would be a poor substitute for the sun. We do not disparage the rush-lights of human reason; but all its guesses and speculations are a poor substitute for the Bible.

How wonderful the light which the Bible casts upon every subject, the knowledge of which is indispensable to salvation! A glory rests on its pages. Christ is the Alpha and the Omega of it. Ruin by the fall, redemption by Christ, regeneration by the Spirit, are here printed in sunbeams. Search it from beginning to end. Search its 40 authors, its 66 books, its 1189 chapters, its 31,173 verses; read its histories, its biographies, its psalms containing the cardiphonia of the Church through all time; read its prophecies, its Gospels, its epistles: every word you read is a ray from the excellent glory. And if it would be true that light had come into the world, although God had revealed no other truth than this, "The blood of Jesus Christ his Son cleanseth us from all sin;" with what refulgence of light are we surrounded as the case stands, and how fearful will be the condemnation of those who love the darkness rather than light, because their deeds are evil!

3. Its *power*. "Where the word of a king is,

there is power." "Is not my Word like a fire, saith the Lord, and like a hammer that breaketh the rock in pieces?" Eighteen hundred years ago, this word, like a grain of mustard seed, was planted in the soil of Judea. It grew, and became a great spreading tree. It made converts in Antioch and Ephesus—in learned Athens, gorgeous Corinth, proud Rome. It will go on in its triumphant march till it conquer the world. Its power is wonderful. When wielded by the Spirit's arm, it is "sharper than a two-edged sword, piercing even to the dividing asunder of soul and spirit." Hence the preacher of the Word occupies a wholly different position from the mere reasoner or disputant of the world.

This is a *convincing* power. Christ only spoke a word at the well, and the woman of Samaria cried, "He told me all things that ever I did." All the sins of her life passed in pale procession before her conscience's eye.

It is an *awakening* power;—so that he who aforetime was fast asleep and profoundly indifferent about Divine things, now starts up to cry, "What must I do to be saved?"

It is a *drawing* power. The iron gate of the heart is unbarred, and opens to receive the King of glory.

It is a *life-giving* power;—so that by a single word, a principle of life is implanted in the soul which makes it a new creature—a principle which all the strength of corruption and all the craft of Satan cannot extinguish—a principle which will grow, till at last, through great tribulation, the pilgrim reaches Mount Zion, the city of the living God, the heavenly Jerusalem. This point is strikingly illustrated by the experience of the Moravian missionaries in Greenland. They tried to civilize the people before giving them the gospel. They continued this plan for twenty years. No sensible effect followed. One day, as one of the missionaries was writing a fair copy of a translation of one of the Gospels, a crowd of natives gathered around him anxious to know the contents of the book. He read to them the history of Christ's sufferings and death. "How was that?" said one of the savages, stepping up to the table, with his voice trembling with emotion. "How was that, tell me once more, for I too would fain be saved?" "These words," writes the missionary, "the like of which I had never heard from a Greenlander, pierced my very soul; and, with tears in my eyes, I related to them the whole history of the sufferings of Christ, and the counsel of God for our salvation. The man who put the question was the first-fruits of Greenland to Christ."

4. Its *depth*. "Thy thoughts are very deep." You can extract the pith of any human book by reading it once or twice. After one or two perusals, you hardly think of reading it again. Even the profoundest book, where you feel at every step in contact with a master mind, may be mastered by severe and strenuous application. But the more you study the Bible, the more do you see its amazing depths, the more do you discover abysses beyond sounding in the ocean of Divine truth. The more deeply you study, the more readily will you join in Agur's confession, "Surely I am more brutish than any man, and have not the understanding of a man: I neither learned wisdom, nor have the knowledge

of the holy." You will ever descry new wonders, new depths which the angels desire to look into, new glories, greater than ever Adam beheld in Paradise. Romaine tells that after studying the Bible on his knees for forty years, he found himself a babe at the end.

5. Its *universal adaptation*. Some books are suited only to a particular age; and when that is past, they are obsolete. Some, that please in childhood, are insipid in riper years. Some are called forth by special circumstances, and are afterwards laid on the shelf to rest. But the Bible is adapted to all, everywhere, in every stage of life, and in every age of the world.* It

---

* I gladly enrich my page with the following passage from the Rev. J. Oswald Dykes' exquisite monogram, "On the Written Word," pp. 33, 34: "As in a wide and varied country, where hills rise from the champaign and woods diversify the open field; in which there grow, not only fruits for food, but flowers too of scent and beauty; where you may lose yourself in nooks of greenery or breathe the cool breezes on the heath, loiter if you will by snug lane sides and in the meadow by the brook, or from the height survey far reaches of the land, till in the blue you catch the gleam of a remoter sea: so may one roam the pages of this book. Long tracts of narrative are broken by bits of poetic elevation; some is bare and some is luscious; from the homely fields where Ruth gleans, we sweep into

delights us in childhood; and it equally delights us when gray hairs find us on the verge of the tomb. It never grows old. Those who embrace it are never behind the age. You may pass with this wondrous book from Europe to Africa, from Paris to Pekin, from Ethiopia to Greenland, from the Atlantic to the Southern Sea: among all these peoples it supplies the want felt by every soul, and in its adaptation to them all you find a new fulfilment of Paul's words,

Ezekiel's rapt vision of unearthly things; we moralize with Solomon and argue with St. Paul; pictures of terror and of peace alternate; there is the national lyric, the battle-song, and the marriage ode; a drama like that of Job, which searches the mysteries of life and death, and letters familiar as those of St. John to Gaius and the elect lady; hymns, prayers, speeches, sermons, official papers, threnodies, pastorals, encyclical letters; all forms of written language which reflect men's parti-colored life, whether in nomad's tent, or city palaces, or the temple of a nation's faith, are turned here into vehicles for the heavenly Word, which God is to quicken in the hearts of men.—Eastern and Western thought meet only in this volume. . . . In a variety so rich as this, each man finds his portion. Young Christians rush along the ardent lines of St. Paul; but in many a corner of the Psalms the devout afflicted soul will nestle, pressing sweetness from each tender word.—The Oriental luxuriates in the sensuousness of the song and in imagery familiar to every Semitic tongue; while Western

"Where there is neither Greek nor Jew, circumcision nor uncircumcision, barbarian, Scythian, bond, nor free: but Christ is all and in all." The soul of the negro slave receives from it the same impression as did the soul of Isaac Newton. The lofty intelligence of the one and the stupidity of the other have at least one great thought in common. The Bible reveals the cross; and the cross illumines all. "Thy testimonies are wonderful."

Christendom has built up its system on the logic of apostles. To plain readers the main drift lies on the surface not to be overlooked; but scientific commentators have work enough to do to fetch side-lights from every part of human knowledge to light up obscure texts,—as well as to trace throughout the whole its unity of plan and the evolution of doctrine; while profounder students still detect endless undercurrents of thought, hints which point out into the unrevealed, and peaks of mystical outlook from which may be descried an ocean of divine truth stretching round as yet by us unvisitable. Why should not God's Book be for all God's children? Is he not rich enough, and his truth large enough, and human speech plastic enough? Blessed be God that his Word has been made to trickle through so many runnels, so that it may the more easily enter and fill the fuller any soul whom he hath made! Blessed be God that his Book is of all books the most marvellously all-sided, the most universally attractive, and the most intensely human!"

We close by indicating *three practical uses:*

1st. *Study the Bible daily.* Read it early in the morning. It was not at nine o'clock in the evening that Israel gathered the manna. No one breakfasts at that hour. Read it all through. When I receive a letter from a friend, I read it from beginning to end. Read it as a wife reads a letter from her husband. Look at the matter historically, and you will find that the Bible has been the *vade mecum*, the counsellor, the delight of saints in all ages. "Oh, sir, what are you doing," writes Romaine to a young friend, "that other books are so much read, and the Bible so neglected? I saw my folly twenty-two years ago, and have since studied little else. You can't read it too much. *Wear it out in reading.*"

2d. *Pray for the Spirit to grave it on your heart with a pen of iron.* When he comes, the Bible becomes a new book, and carries its own evidence along with it. Until he comes it is a sealed book. Every time you open the Bible say, "Open thou mine eyes that I may behold wondrous things out of thy law!"

3d. *Practise it daily.* The way to *see* aright is to *do* aright. Follow this light and it will guide to heaven.

> "Yon cottager, who weaves at her own door,
> Pillows and bobbins all her little store :
> Content, though mean, and cheerful if not gay,
> Shuffling her threads about the livelong day ;
> Just earns a scanty pittance, and at night
> Lies down secure, her heart and pocket light ;
> She, for her humble sphere by nature fit,
> Has little understanding and no wit,
> Receives no praise : but, though her lot be such
> (Toilsome and indigent), she renders much ;
> Just knows and knows no more her Bible true,
> A truth the brilliant Frenchman never knew,
> And in that charter reads with sparkling eyes
> Her title to a treasure in the skies."

XII.

TAKE HEED HOW YE HEAR.

LUKE viii. 18.
"Take heed therefore how ye hear."

IN the parish of Ferintosh in Ross-shire, there lived in the last age a very holy minister named Charles Calder. He sowed precious seed there for thirty-eight years. He walked with God, and God took him in the year 1812. His memory is still fragrant in Ross-shire and beyond it. Let me tell you of a good old man, who was long one of his hearers.

William Tolmie was the beadle in the parish. He was an earnest hearer of the Word. He was accustomed to hear for eternity. Even in his old age, his venerable figure was always seen on the pulpit stairs. The bent form, the long white locks, the antique costume, and the solemn look caught the eye. It was once the writer's privilege to preach in the Burn of Ferintosh. The Burn is a hallowed spot. It is shaped like a vast amphitheatre. The congregation assemble there on the Communion Sabbath. As many as ten and even fifteen thousand have often assembled there. The tables are spread in the centre, and God's children gather round and partake of the sacred feast. What days of power there have been in that spot! How many sinners have been converted there, and how many saints have there seen the King in his beauty, and the land that is very far off!

After the sermon, William came up and said, "You reminded me of what I heard from Mr. Calder nine and thirty years ago." "What was that?" said the writer. "Well," said he, in slow, solemn tones, "the last day he stood in yon pulpit, as he closed his sermon, he looked round the congregation, and said, 'I have an impression, either that I am speaking to-day or some of you hearing for the last time; and before we part for ever, I shall call five great witnesses to avouch that I have declared unto you the whole counsel of God. The first is God the Father, the omniscient and heart-searching God. I call him to witness that I have set before you life and death. The second is God the Son. I call him to witness that he himself has been the burden of my preaching during these thirty-eight years. The third is God the Holy Spirit. I call him to witness that I have set before you the nature, marks, and fruits of his work, and the necessity of the new birth. The fourth great witness is the Bible. And the fifth is the company of the elect angels, who are now waiting to rejoice over your conversion. And I call your own consciences—I call the stones and timbers of this house to witness, that I have not shunned to declare unto you the whole counsel of God! 'If any man love not the Lord Jesus Christ, let him be Anathema Maranatha.' Then," said William (whose eyes were full with the memory of the scene), "he closed the Bible, and came down the pulpit stairs, and never went up."

Dear young friends, would you not like to be such hearers as William Tolmie? We have few such. He sat like Mary at Jesus' feet, and hearkened to his word. He kept it in a sanctified memory. He remembered it as long as he lived.

The object of this chapter is to teach you to do likewise.

There are three bad classes of hearers now,—just as there were in Jesus' day—wayside hearers, stony-ground hearers, and thorny-ground hearers—and only one good class. Three bad classes to one good. "Take heed therefore how ye hear."

This subject is very seasonable in times of revival. One mark of revival is that people hear then with an earnestness which they never knew before. They flock to the house of God, and drink in the Word as thirsty fields drink the falling rain. Multitudes of young persons like you, have begun to hear in this way within the last few years. Perhaps some of your companions are of the number. They have found Jesus. You saw their joy when they found him. You remember with what gladness they sang from overflowing hearts :

> "Happy day, happy day,
> When Jesus washed my sins away :
> He taught me how to watch and pray,
> And live rejoicing every day :
> Happy day, happy day,
> When Jesus washed my sins away!"

It is a solemn thing to live through a time of revival. For several years the Holy Spirit has, at intervals, been working with unwonted power in our land. On many spots showers of blessing have fallen. We may never see such years again.

The question, How is the Word to be read and heard, that it may become effectual to salvation, is answered in the Shorter Catechism as follows: "That the Word may become effectual to salvation, we must attend thereunto with diligence, preparation, and prayer : receive it with faith and love, lay it up in our hearts, and practise it in our lives."

What a beautiful photograph of the way in

which men hear the Word in times of awakening! Dear young friends, you have seen every line of it verified. Let us examine it carefully. Thou who didst open Lydia's heart, open the hearts of the writer and the reader!

I. We must hear with *diligence*, or *earnestness:*

1. Because *God is the speaker*. The God who made you, who holds your breath in his hand, who will one day be your Judge, speaks to you in the gospel. The still, small voice you hear is God's. If you would listen earnestly to some great one of the earth, and reckon it condescension in him to speak to you, how much more earnestly should you listen to the great God! "See that ye refuse not him that speaketh: for if they escaped not who refused him that spake on earth, much more shall not we escape if we turn away from him that speaketh from heaven." "O earth, earth, earth, hear the Word of the Lord!" Ministers are but the voice. God is the speaker. Elijah wrapped his face in his mantle when he heard God speak. One of the great errors of our day consists in forgetting

this. Thousands hear the Word as the word of man. They do not see God's authority stamped upon it. They forget that it is "full of majesty." They go home and say, "We heard Mr. A.,—pretty good, but fallen off, awkward manner, nothing to Guthrie:" or, "We heard Dr. B.,—very deep, reads very closely, the people could not follow him." What a contrast to such words as these—"Speak, Lord, for thy servant heareth." "I will hear what God the Lord will speak." "O Lord, I have heard thy speech, and was afraid."

2. Because the preached Word is *God's ordinance to save you*. Your eternal interest depends on your hearing it "with diligence." If you are not saved by it, you will never be saved. Every offer of Christ is a cord of love to draw you to his cross. Every sermon is a chain of gold let down from the Throne that you may take hold of it and live. A deaf man, they say, hears the clink of money. The unsearchable riches of Christ are offered you. God sends us with the gospel to open your eyes and to turn you from darkness to light. "We

are ambassadors for Christ, as though God did beseech you by us: we pray you in Christ's stead, be ye reconciled to God."

3. Because the Word, *if not a savor of life unto life, is a savor of death unto death.* No speech is more common than this—"We can't be the worse of hearing a good sermon." The Bible asserts the contrary. "The preaching of the cross is to them that perish foolishness." "To you which believe he is precious; but unto them which be disobedient . . . he is a stone of stumbling, and a rock of offence." Christ came "for judgment into this world, that they who see not might see, and that they who see might be made blind." When you hear the Word then, think, "My salvation perhaps depends upon this sermon." "This may be Christ's last knock at my door!" "This may be the deciding day!" Let the awful interests at stake arouse you to hear with the ears of your heart! No ruin is so sore as the ruin of gospel despisers. You pity the heathen. Many among us, it is to be feared, will sink into a darker hell than they. Why? Because of a

despised gospel. The man who falls from a little height is scarcely hurt; the man who falls from a steeple is killed. The writer knew of a youth, the son of a godly mother, who ran a swift career of profligacy, and was suddenly cut down. "Oh, if I could cut out of my heart the bit on which my poor mother's neglected counsels are written!" were his last words. "Woe unto thee, Chorazin! woe unto thee, Bethsaida! for if the mighty works which were done in you had been done in Tyre and Sidon, they would have repented long ago in sackcloth and ashes. And thou, Capernaum, which art exalted unto heaven, shalt be brought down to hell."

The want of diligence in hearing is a painful topic, which we would fain pass over. Many are all activity during the week, and all indolence on the Sabbath. Many attend church only once who could easily attend twice. They will not hearken to the voice of the charmer charming ever so sweetly. The slightest excuse keeps them at home. Many members of churches would be startled at the year's end if they were told the number of diets from which they were absent during the year. The weather is the great excuse with young and old. Sabbath is wet; they look out in the morning, and decide that it would be a serious risk to venture to church. They stay at home. The sermon which might have been blessed to their conversion, is preached to the empty pew. Monday is wet; they look out (for we don't speak of the aged and infirm) and decide that it will clear up by mid-day: then business is business; they have engagements of pressing importance with this person and that person; and away they rush into the din of the world. Did you ever hear of a shopkeeper not taking down his shutters, or a merchant staying at home from his office, or a tradesman from his work because the day was wet? When the Spirit comes, people never think of weather or distance. "Take heed how you hear."

II. Hear with *preparation*.

You believe that the preacher must prepare —must seek by meditation and prayer to "find out acceptable words "—" words as goads, and as nails fastened by the masters of assemblies." You believe that anxious days and nights are not too much for this. You believe, too, that the hearer ought to prepare for a communion Sabbath, and to ponder, as he approaches the table, the words: "Loose thy shoes from off thy feet, for the place whereon thou standest is holy." The hearer ought to prepare for *every* Sabbath. The soil as well as the seed must be prepared. It must be torn up and cleared of stones and weeds. "Break up your fallow ground—it is time to seek the Lord." True preaching requires two to be divinely prepared —the preacher and the hearer. A good hearer is as rare as a good preacher. The preacher should stick to his text—till he gets into its heart, and opens up its richness, and sweetness, and heavenliness; but the hearer should stick to it too.

Banish the world's cares, if you would be prepared to hear. The Sabbath is the Christian's busiest day.

> "O time of tranquil joy, and holy feeling!
> When over earth God's Spirit from above
> Spreads out his wings of love!
> When sacred thoughts, like angels, come appealing
> To our tent-doors; O eve, to earth and heaven
> The sweetest of the seven!
>
> "How peaceful are thy skies! thy air is clearer,
> As on the advent of a gracious time;
> The sweetness of its prime
> Blesseth the world, and Eden's days seem nearer;
> I hear, in each faint stirring of the breeze,
> God's voice among the trees."—J. D. BURNS.

He rises early, as Jesus rose early from the dead. He casts the world's cares aside, as he casts aside his working-clothes. "Abide ye here," he says, "while I go and worship yonder." He seeks special grace to tune his soul, so that, like Daniel, he may "kneel upon his knees, with his windows open toward Jerusalem." He gets his children and servants ready betimes for the house of prayer, so as not to enter late, and disturb the service. "We are all here present before God," said Cornelius, "to hear all things that are commanded thee of God." And if worldly cares return to eat the life out of his service, he does as Abraham when "the fowls came down upon the carcasses, and he drove them away." "Vain world!" he says, "thou hast had six days entire: little enough if one is devoted to the things of eternity!"* How completely were the three thousand weaned from the world on the day of Pentecost! "Continuing daily with one accord in the temple, and breaking bread from house to house, they did eat their meat with gladness and singleness of heart, praising God."

---

* "While Mr. Stewart (of Cromarty) staid at the castle, he told an anecdote which the duchess often repeated with great animation: Hector Munro was a half-witted man; but, like so many of the weak in this world, he was strong in the grace that is in Christ Jesus. Mr. Stewart having invited him to pay him a visit at Cromarty Manse, he came most inopportunely on the Saturday afternoon, with the design of remaining all night, when the minister was busily engaged with his work for the Sabbath. . . . Hector having come in his best clothes, Mr. Stewart addressed him, 'Weel, Hector, ye've made yersel' braw the day.' 'Hoot ay,' said Hector, 'folk maks themsel's braw to gang to thae vain markets: but I'se warrant the Sabbath's the best market, for it's there we get without money and without price. An', Maister Stewart, I'm thinkin' the Saturday's jist like the Christian's deathbed: he's dune his wark, an' he's washed, an' he's clean, an' he lies doon, an' he waukens— an' it's the Sabbath! An' He was braw himsel' that day.'"— *Life of the last Duchess of Gordon*, p. 167.

"*Wash your hands in innocency.*" The laver in the tabernacle stood between the door and the altar. The priests washed in it ere they approached the altar on pain of death. All believers are now made kings and priests to God. Wash in the laver, ere you go to hear the Word of God.

> "There is a fountain filled with blood,
> Drawn from Emmanuel's veins;
> And sinners plunged beneath that flood
> Lose all their guilty stains."

"Lay apart all filthiness, and superfluity of naughtiness, and receive with meekness the ingrafted Word." There is no true hearing without washing in the blood. There is no coming to Mount Zion without coming to the blood of sprinkling. Prize this blood. Wash in it, that you may be cleansed from dead works. Without the constant application of it, ordinances increase your guilt. The ark among the Philistines made the Lord visit them with plagues. If you go to hear God's Word without banishing the cares of the world, wherein do you differ from the money-changers that Jesus drove out of the temple? You offer but the dead carcass of a sacrifice. If you go without washing in the blood, Satan's black seal is upon you. "Take heed how ye hear."

III. Hear with *prayer*.

When the General Assembly of 1859 welcomed Mr. Brownlow North as an evangelist, he gave an address which stirred the hearts of thousands, and made many gray-haired fathers weep. The key-note was: "There is one special thing for which God is very angry with Scotland, and for which his Spirit is so little among us; and that is, *the neglect of united prayer*, which is God's *appointed means for bringing down the Holy Spirit*. You find congregations of fourteen hundred or sixteen hundred, on the Sunday, and at the prayer-meeting twenty or thirty persons! The Scotch are a sermon-hearing rather than a praying people." Dear young friends, we appeal specially to you on this point. Prayer-meetings have been, in every age, the great means of opening heaven's windows. In 1742, ninety heads of families sent Mr. M'Culloch of Cambuslang a request to open such a meeting. Soon after there was a "great rain." M'Cheyne tells that, on his return from the Holy Land, there were *thirty-nine* weekly prayer-meetings in his congregation, and five of them entirely conducted by children. Who can tell the blessings that these solemn prayer-meetings in Glasgow, in the Free Assembly Hall, Edinburgh, and elsewhere, have brought down upon the world!

If three hundred praying men and women assembled in a church, like Gideon's three hundred, whose watchword was, "The sword of the Lord and of Gideon," happy the minister who is in the pulpit. There's no support like the prayers of God's people. A praying people make a preaching minister. Neither great gifts, nor hard study, nor notes in the book, will avail without the people's prayers. He who is best supported in this way will be most successful in winning souls. The model hearer hears and prays, like the gardener who, on being asked what he was doing, replied, "I am digging and praying." Oh! if every hearer came from his knees with the dew of the holy Ghost upon his soul, it would be easy to preach then. Moses' hands were steady when Aaron and Hur stood beside him. They would not have been steady if Aaron and Hur had deserted him. It's a cruel thing to hear a minister without praying for him.

Pray, then, when you hear. Pray that the King of kings may be seen riding gloriously on his white horse. Pray for *yourself*, and say, "I am a poor dying sinner; Lord, open my eyes that of thy law the wonders I may see." Pray for your *families*, that they may stand at last in unbroken companies with the Lamb on Mount Zion. Pray for *ministers*, that they may have the unction from the Holy One, and the tongue of fire. Pray for *God's children*, that they may be revived as the corn, and that, like Naphtali, they may be "satisfied with favor, and full with the blessing of the Lord." Pray for *all the churches* of Christ, that they may "have rest and be edified, walking in the fear of the Lord, and in the comfort of the Holy Ghost." Pray for the *young*, that they may seek and find Jesus now, like one who found him lately, and said, "There's glory in my heart now." Pray for *Sabbath-schools*, that they may be nurseries of the Church below, and of the Church above, and that in all the classes there may be found groups of the lambs of Jesus. Pray for *sinners* in your own congregation, whether they be open sinners or cold formalists, that they may be awakened to seek the Lord weeping. Pray for *non-church-goers*, that they may see the worth of divine ordinances, and be taught to say before they die, "How amiable are thy tabernacles, O Lord! A day in thy courts is better than a thousand." Oh, if God would pour out the Spirit of prayer on every hearer, what life, and light, and power —what solemnity—what Bethel-like fear—would be felt in all the services!

A sovereign will grant the prayer of a petition signed by a whole community, when he would not grant the prayer of an individual. So with God. He cannot refuse the united prayers of his children who cry day and night unto him. When the one hundred and twenty prayed in the upper room at Jerusalem, the Spirit came down like a rushing mighty wind. Soon after, "when they had prayed, the place was shaken where they were assembled together, and they were all filled with the Holy Ghost, and they spake the Word of God with boldness, . . . and with great power gave the apostles witness of the resurrection of the Lord Jesus: and great grace was upon them all." "Give ear, O Shepherd of Israel, thou that leadest Joseph like a flock, thou that dwellest between the cherubim, shine forth." "Awake, O north wind; and come, thou south: blow upon my garden, that the spices thereof may flow out. Let my beloved come into his garden, and eat his pleasant fruits."

IV. We must *receive* the Word heard with *faith*.

Receive. A lady heard the same sermon thrice from the late Dr. Macdonald. She met him one evening, and tried to talk merrily of the circumstance. "What was the text?" said the doctor. She told him. "What were the heads?" After some hesitation she told them, though not in the correct order. "What were the leading thoughts?" Not a word. "You have much need of hearing it a fourth time," said the doctor. Hundreds of sermons are lost in this way. The very text is forgotten. A silly story sticks in an unsanctified memory; holy truth oozes out of it. Ezekiel's photograph of the hearers of his day resembles many hearers in ours. "They come unto thee as the people cometh, and they sit before thee as my people, and they hear thy words, but they will not do them; for with their mouth they show much love, but their heart goeth after their covetousness. And, lo, thou art unto them as a very lovely song of one that hath a pleasant voice, and can play well on an instrument; for they hear thy words, but they do them not." (Ezek. xxxiii. 31, 32.) "Therefore we ought to give the more earnest heed to the things which we have heard, lest at any time we should let them slip."

With *Faith*. Learn the vital worth of faith in hearing from Heb. iv. 2—"The word preached did not profit them, not being mixed with faith in them that heard it." Many who heard the gospel from Jesus' own lips, only sank into a darker death; because the Word was not mixed with faith in their hearts. Faith is the eye with which you see the cross. Faith is the hand with which you grasp the cross. Faith is the mouth with which you "eat Christ's flesh and drink his blood." No faith, no Christ. No Christ, no life. See, then, the evil of unbelief; it makes the Word preached worse than vain. "Oh that thou hadst known the things which belong to thy peace: but now they are hid from thine eyes!"

Objection: "But I have faith." Is it true? For true faith in these two facts—I am a great sinner, and Christ is a great Saviour—will save the soul. Is it true? For many mistake the assent of the understanding for the consent of the heart. Boston tells that he met a person in his household visitations who said she had believed all her days. In June, 1859, when all Ulster was shaking like the valley of dry bones, a man of outwardly stainless life in Coleraine was pricked to the heart, and cried bitterly for mercy. "Oh, John," said his wife, "ye had faith afore!" "The devils believe and tremble."

Question: "How shall I know that my faith is true?" In two ways—(1.) True faith is the "*substance of things hoped for*, the evidence of things not seen." It gives reality to its objects. It sees a real God, a real Christ, a real heaven, a real hell, where the world sees nothing. The love of God—the preciousness of the blood of Christ—the dreadful evil of sin—the solemn cries of a death-bed—the great gulf between Christ and the wicked when they die—are realities now. "The Judge stands at the door." The view which a child of God has of spiritual things is far more different from the world's view of them than the picture of a man from the living man himself. How? Because Christ declares, "The men of the old world *knew* not until the flood came and took them all away." They had often heard it. Yes—just as thoughtless sinners have often heard of hell. But they *knew* it not.

(2.) True faith *appropriates these unseen realities*. It links the soul to them. It lives on them. "I live by faith," says Paul. It's my only means of support. Moses left Egypt because he saw God invisible as *his* God. Not a promise but faith says, "Amen, Lord, to that promise." It hungers and thirsts after righteousness. It waits at the posts of Christ's door. Thus it transforms the soul. Head faith, again, like a bucket without a bottom, draws up nothing.

V. We must receive the Word with *love*.

We once travelled on board a steamer with a venerable minister. He had a rich fund of anecdote, and the wide range of his information made him a charming fellow-traveller. Suddenly, as we were deep in talk, he turned away, and pulled an old letter out of his pocket, and began to read. "What paper is this?" we asked. "It's a letter from my wife," said he. "You seem to have read it pretty well." "Yes," he replied, "I have read it, and read it, and I am reading it yet again." The Bible is such a letter to the child of God. It's a letter from home. Every time he reads it he sees some new glory in it. "It is the voice of my

Beloved." "This command (says an old writer) is a secret of Jesus, this promise the sweet voice of Jesus, these consolations the comforts of Jesus, these ministers the messengers of Jesus, these ordinances the kingdom of Jesus." Hence the love of God's children for the preached Word. "Lord, I have loved the habitation of thy house, and the place where thine honor dwelleth." "I was glad when they said unto me, Let us go into the house of the Lord." David envied the very swallows that built about the temple.

On sacramental occasions in the Highlands, the congregation assemble on the hill-side. Sometimes they may be seen carrying forms, chairs, stools, to the hallowed spot. There they sit, wet or dry, during the five days of the solemnity, with a reverence and a love for God's ordinances rarely equalled. One sacramental Monday evening, walking along the principal street in Stornoway, we met a frail old figure, carrying a stool in his hand. "What have you got here, Alister?" "Oh," said he, with tears, "my heart was sore taking the stool away!"

There had Alister during these days been refreshed with draughts from the well of Bethlehem. There had he taken the cup of salvation. He felt it good to be there. It was the gate of heaven. He was wedded to the spot. He wept taking the stool away.

When God revealed his glory at Cambuslang in 1742, some declared that they would not for a world have been absent. Others said, Now let thy servants depart in peace on this very spot, for our eyes have seen Thy salvation. They would fain never have returned to the world again. And during the late time of refreshing, how many in Glasgow and Edinburgh, Dumfries and Perth, Aberdeen and Huntly, were filled with such joy that they could wish for the tongues of angels, to sing their Redeemer's praises! "That blessed sound of prayers and psalms," said one, "put me in mind of the sweet songs that are sung at God's right hand!" Dear young friends, may you never forget what your own eyes have seen of God's glorious power!

VI. We must *lay the Word up* in our hearts.

If the Word has brought life to your soul, you will be in no danger of forgetting it. Sooner will your right hand forget its cunning. One has found peace from the words, "Behold the Lamb of God;" another from, "Yet there is room;" and still another from the words, "The blood of Jesus Christ cleanseth us from all sin:" and these words are treasured up in your heart's core. "I will never forget thy precepts, for by them thou hast quickened me." "Thy Word have I hid in my heart, that I might not sin against thee." Dear young friends, be like the Bereans who searched the Scriptures daily. Remember what you hear. Harrow in the seed by meditation. Glean in the field of the Word, that you may have something for those at home. Gather up the fragments that nothing be lost.

But, lest we sadden the heart of any drooping disciple who has no memory, let us state a case which Mr. W. C. Burns, now in glory, told us of. There was a poor widow who loved her Saviour, and often went great distances to hear. Her neighbors scoffed at her. One day, as she was washing worsted in a stream that ran by her cottage, a neighbor came up and said, "Well, you've been at the sacrament." "Yes." "Tell us some of these grand sermons you heard." "I can't." "Do you mind nothing?" "Nothing." "What's the use of going, then?" "Ah!" said she, with beaming face, "look at this worsted. It does not keep any of the running water; but it's getting whiter. So, though my soul keeps but little of the pure waters of the sanctuary, I trust it's getting whiter!"

VII. We must *practise it* in our lives.

It is a common taunt with non-church-goers, "We know many who attend church, and we see little difference between them and ourselves, although we attend no church." Hearers of the Word, wipe this reproach away! Be living epistles of Christ. Take the Bible as your lamp and light all the week. Walk in the truth. Let your conversation be as it becometh the gospel of Christ. You value the ministry of the Word. Let your holy lives be the response to it.

Dear young friends, in conclusion let me say—*Don't let the summer days of youth pass away without giving your hearts to Jesus.* John Angell James observes, in his "Anxious Inquirer," that the great majority of the converted are converted between the ages of fifteen and twenty-five. The tongue of an angel cannot tell the priceless value of these ten years. If you let them pass without finding Jesus, you will never be so likely to find him again. And in Robe's "Narrative," it is said, "Many solid divines are of opinion, that there are but few of those who live under the gospel from their infancy *who are converted after they are thirty years of age.*" May the Holy Spirit draw you to Jesus now!

Let me speak to *the old*, whose eyes may fall upon these lines. We have more hope in addressing the young: but to you also we say, "Take heed how ye hear." We would affectionately ask—

Are you an *irregular* hearer? Do you often stay at home without cause? For when men often stay without cause, they drop away altogether, and become home heathens. You may be one of these yet. Take heed, above all, lest you have cause to reflect bitterly on this when you come to die.

Are you a *wandering* hearer? Our more judicious hearers do not wander. There *is* such a thing as the pastoral tie. It is a tender tie. There is a risk of having itching ears. If every hearer wandered, there would be no congregations. There would only be mere crowds.

Sleeping in church has been the habit of a few from Eutychus downwards. We never heard of legatees sleeping when a rich will was being read. In the gospel we have the last testament of the Son of God.

What should we be without the gospel? There's no famine like a famine of the gospel. Many from abroad cry for it, and say, Come over and help us. Take heed how you hear it.

XIII.

AS WHITE AS SNOW.

Isaiah i. 18.

"Come now, and let us reason together, saith the Lord: though your sins be as scarlet, they shall be as white as snow; though they be red like crimson, they shall be as wool."

WHAT is a beautiful thought of the lamented Dr. James Hamilton's: Suppose that every one were to mark in golden letters the text which has been the means of saving his soul. The apostle Paul would mark the words, "Saul, Saul, why persecutest thou me?" for it was these words spoken by Jesus from the dazzling light that made him a new creature. In the Bible of the Macedonian jailer the golden letters would be found at Acts xvi. 31, "Believe on the Lord Jesus Christ, and thou shalt be saved:" for, embracing this simple offer, he rejoiced believing in God with all his house. Martin Luther would print the text, "The just shall live by faith," in gold: for that text spoken by the gentle lips of the vicar-general guided him to peace; and the young monk of Erfurth, reduced by fasts and tears and struggles to the verge of the grave, found rest in the wounds of Jesus. In the Bible of Bunyan the mark would be found at, "Yet there is room:" it was through the lattice of these words that he first saw the cross, and he thought God had put them into the Bible to meet his special case. And the Ironside soldier would indicate Eccles. xi. 9: for it was there that the bullet stopped which, but for the interposing Bible, would have pierced his bosom; and when the battle was over he read, "Rejoice, O young man, in thy youth, and let thy heart cheer thee in the days of thy youth, and walk in the ways of thine heart, and in the sight of thine eyes; but know thou that for all these things God will bring thee into judgment."* But who can tell how

* "The Lamp and the Lantern," p. 128.

many would inshrine in gold a text which has comforted millions, and is destined to comfort millions more; or what words do we so instinctively turn to in directing anxious souls to Christ as these, "Come now, and let us reason together, saith the Lord: though your sins be as scarlet, they shall be as white as snow; though they be red like crimson, they shall be as wool"? We have here an *invitation* and a *promise*.

1. An *invitation:* "Come now, and let us reason together."

(1.) God is *willing to come to terms.* When a quarrel arises among men, it is not the offended party who first makes proposals of peace. He feels that he has been wronged, and that he has a right to demand satisfaction from the offender. But here the party offended makes offers of peace first. God as it were descends from his throne, and invites the sinner to a conference. The King invites the rebel—the Judge invites the criminal. God has no pleasure in being at war with so insignificant an antagonist as fallen man. He wishes the case to be settled here and now. He is easy to be entreated. The

Father's heart yearns over the prodigal. God is in earnest. He has set up a Throne of grace where he is waiting to be gracious. He stretches out the golden sceptre. The case is easier settled here, ere the day of grace is past, ere it goes up unsettled to the great white throne. "Fury is not in me: who would set the briers and thorns against me in battle? I would go through them, I would burn them together; but let him take hold of my strength, that he may make peace with me: and he shall make peace with me."

(2.) He has *provided an Advocate to plead* for us. We cannot reason ourselves.

In an action where the crown is pursuer, and a wretch laden with crimes is defender, he has little chance. Unskilled in legal forms himself he cannot employ the first counsel—such counsel will not undertake his case, and it is lost. But here, although in legal phrase the King of kings is the pursuer, and guilty man the defender, he has, wonderful to tell, provided the first counsel in heaven to plead for us, an Advocate who *never lost* a case, who never *took a fee* for a case, who never *refused to undertake* a case, however poor and needy the client. Surely one of the great marvels of the gospel! No wonder that we can call this text a star of the first magnitude in the firmament of divine truth. An Advocate is here provided to conduct your case who will go into court with you; who will bring it to a successful issue without fee or reward; who reckons it the greatest joy, that you lay upon him all your sins and intrust him with the whole responsibility of making your peace with God; who glories in being the Mediator, the Reconciler, the Peace-maker between earth and heaven! "We have an Advocate with the Father, Jesus Christ the righteous:" "Wherefore he is able also to save them to the uttermost that come unto God by him, seeing he ever liveth to make intercession for them."

(3.) He *furnishes us with arguments.* His own *name* is one—God is love. Sin-burned, trembling soul! let this name be your plea. There is a perfect universe of tenderness in it.

Christ's *finished work* is another. This plea carries all before it. Satan cannot withstand it.

When Joshua, clad in filthy garments, stood before the angel of the Lord, Satan stood at his right hand to resist him; but when the angel said, "Is not this a brand plucked out of the fire?" Satan fled, and we never read of him more throughout the whole book of Zechariah! However great your sins, the blood of Christ is greater. Although they cry aloud for vengeance, with voice still louder, and sweet as the music of paradise, the blood of sprinkling cries, "Deliver from going down to the pit, I have found a ransom!" The waters of the flood covered the highest mountains. Not one mountain-top could be seen. Looking from above, you could see nothing but a vast world of waters—a mighty expanse reflecting the beams of the sun. So if you are covered with the righteousness of Christ, the mountains of your sins will not be seen.

The *promises* are another. They hang in golden clusters.

God's *welcome to penitents* in all ages is another. Said Benhadad's servants (1 Kings xx. 31): "We have heard that the kings of the house of Israel are merciful kings," and with sackcloth on their loins and ropes on their heads they came to the king of Israel, and obtained mercy for their fallen master. Thus, looking over the archives of his government, the countless roll of sinners, like you and me, whom he has pardoned with overflowing love from Manasseh down to the sinner who has found mercy to-day—may you reason, "Lord, I have heard that thou showest mercy to thousands, that thy mercy is like a river still running, and I have come to taste of it."

Observe the word *now*. "Come *now*." Not to-morrow. "The Holy Ghost saith, To-day." God offers to reason with man. He has fixed the place—the mercy-seat, and the time—now. He is waiting. Jesus is knocking. The Holy Spirit is striving. The great gospel is appealing. Now may be the eleventh hour. Death is at the door.

An artist requested permission to paint a portrait of the Queen. The request was granted. The time and place were fixed. At the fixed place and time her majesty appeared; but the artist was not there; he was busy making preparations. In a few minutes he arrived, and found that the Queen had left and would not return.

Thus many lose the supreme opportunity. The old world lost its day. Esau lost his day, and bitter cries could not recall it. Israel in the wilderness lost their day, and God sware in his wrath that they should not enter into his rest. Jerusalem lost her day, and Jesus wept over her. The foolish virgins lost their day, and were only awakened, as a great writer expresses it, by "the bridal train sweeping by, and the shutting of the doors, and the discovery that their lamps were gone out." Felix lost his day. And remember well, many a day has begun fair, and continued long so, that has had a foul evening.

> "The voice of wisdom cries, Be in time;
> To give up every sin, in earnest now begin;
> The night will soon set in, Be in time.
>
> "Oh should the door be shut when you come;
> Should God in thunder say, Depart from me away,
> 'Twill be in vain to pray, Be in time."

2. A *promise:* "Though your sins be as scarlet, they shall be as white as snow."

However great and heinous, however red and bloody, your sins be—and though they be countless as the sand of the sea—they will all be blotted out, they will all be forgiven and forgotten by a gracious God. The sin of your nature, the sin of your heart, the sin of your life, the sin of your lips, your secret sins hid from every eye but God's—all your sins and iniquities, and unrighteousnesses, and transgressions, will be *made as white as snow.*

(1.) Every *sin has the color of scarlet and crimson.* A deep-red bloody color. In heaven's statute-book sin is a capital crime. We call murder a capital crime because it spills the life of the body. Cain's hands are still red with his brother's blood. But sin spills the life of the soul. Nay more, it strikes a blow at the crown, at the very being of God. Hence "the wages of sin is *death.*"

(2.) The word translated "scarlet" means a *double dye*—a deeper, darker dye. "Though your sins be as scarlet;" though you be stained not only with original depravity, but doubly stained with actual transgression, in thought, word, and deed—though you be steeped and soaking in sin like cloth in a vat of scarlet dye—though your life be one web of sin, the woof of your daily transgressions interwoven with the warp of your original corruption—the moment you are sprinkled with the precious blood you become as white as snow.

We once visited a famous dyeing establishment. Inspecting the various processes, we were surprised at the strange transformations of material from gray to gold, and from the pale white of the lily to the red of the fresh blown rose. "Can you extract scarlet and crimson?" we asked. "Yes." "Will the material be white thereafter?" "No; we can extract the colors, but the material will be clay-colored, or yellowish-gray." A familiar fact in nature gave us a fresh insight into another fact in grace. It gave us a fresh discovery of the preciousness of that blood which not only extracts the scarlet and the crimson of our sins, but makes the vilest sinner as *white as snow.**

This fact is the pith and core of the gospel. Jesus took our sins; we receive his righteousness. He paid our debts; we receive a discharge in full. He died our death; we live his life. God does not ask two lives, or two deaths, or two payments. Christ suffered the sentence of

---

* "I remember well how once God preached to me by a similitude in the depth of winter. The earth had been black, and there was scarcely a green thing or a flower to be seen. As you looked across the field, there was nothing but blackness—bare hedges and leafless trees, and black, black earth—wherever you looked. On a sudden God spake, and unlocked the treasures of the snow, and white flakes descended until there was no blackness to be seen, for all was one sheet of dazzling whiteness. It was at that time I was seeking the Saviour, and it was then I found him; and I remember well that Sermon which I saw before me. 'Come now, and let us reason together: though your sins be as scarlet, they shall be as white as snow; though they be red like crimson, they shall be as wool.' Sinner, thy heart is like that black ground; thy soul is like that bare tree and hedgerow, without leaf or blossom: God's grace is like the white snow. It shall fall upon thee till thy doubting heart shall glitter in whiteness of pardon, and thy poor black soul shall be covered with the spotless purity of the Son of God. He seems to say to you, Sinner, you are black, but I am ready to forgive you; I will wrap thy heart in the ermine of my Son's righteousness, and with my Son's own garments on, thou shalt be holy as the Holy One."—*Spurgeon.*

the law, and the law cannot touch us when we hide under the canopy of his glorious mediatorhood. His cross is the payment of our penalty, the cancelling of our debt, the tearing up of the bond or handwriting which was against us. When his blood is sprinkled upon us, we become partakers of his death, we die in him, we undergo the sentence of the law in him,—and then the guilt passes away. We are counted in law, and treated by God, as men who have paid the whole penalty and been "washed from their sins in his blood." Though our sins were as scarlet, they are as white as snow; though they were red like crimson, they are as wool.

We close with an extract beautifully illustrative of our subject from the life of the last Duchess of Gordon: "One night as she lay sleepless, there appeared as if really before her eyes a white scroll unrolled, glistening with unearthly brightness, and with floods of vivid light ever flowing over it. Written at the head of the scroll in large bright letters of gold, she read this inscription, 'The Lord our righteousness.' All her darkness was dispelled in a moment, and by the glorious words the Spirit imprinted on her heart and conscience the fresh seal of the pardon of all her sins, she believed and knew that Jesus was made of God unto her righteousness, and that his blood had made her whiter than snow. Her soul entered in a moment into perfect rest; and she rejoiced in the full assurance that for her to die that night was to depart and be forever with the Lord."

XIV.

THE GREAT MULTITUDE.

Rev. vii. 9-17.

"After this I beheld, and, lo, a great multitude which no man could number, of all nations, and kindreds, and people, and tongues, stood before the throne, and before the Lamb, clothed with white robes, and palms in their hands; and cried with a loud voice, saying, Salvation to our God which sitteth upon the throne, and unto the Lamb. . . . These are they which came out of great tribulation, and have washed their robes, and made them white in the blood of the Lamb. . . . They shall hunger no more, neither thirst any more; neither shall the sun light on them, nor any heat. For the Lamb, which is in the midst of the throne, shall feed them, and shall lead them unto living fountains of waters; and God shall wipe away all tears from their eyes."

LATE in the afternoon, when the tired laborer raises his bended back and sees the sun wheeling to the west, he comforts himself with the thought that evening is coming, and that he will soon get home to rest. The tempest-tossed mariner feels his heart beat quicker as he descries the hill-tops of his native shore rising out of the sea. And the soldier, during the weary night-watch in the bivouac, when the distant hum of men and the random shot tell of possible death on the morrow, solaces himself with the dream of home, the loving welcomes, and the joy of recounting his perils and hair-breadth escapes.

It is with some such feeling that we read these words. The home-sick *will* think of home. Here is the home of the redeemed—the home of the faithful laborer, of the heavenward-bound voyager, of the good soldier of Jesus Christ. We have vivid life-like glimpses of heaven in such words as those—"To-day thou shalt be with me in paradise;" "Having a desire to depart, and to be with Christ, which is far better." But in the Apocalypse the veil is drawn aside, heaven's crystal doors are thrown open, and the beloved disciple, like the shepherds Bunyan saw on the Delectable Mountains, carries us away to the top of a great and high mountain, and shows us, through the glass of faith, the glories of the New Jerusalem. Here we have—

1. *A vision of the redeemed.*

John tells us he saw a great multitude of all nations, and kindreds, and people, and tongues. We are apt to think the saints are few, and, like Elijah in his fit of despondency, we sometimes make them fewer than they are. We are apt to confine our regards to our own country, perhaps to our own church. We are here assured that when the saints of all ages and lands are gathered together, they will form a multitude innumerable as the stars of night, as the sand upon the sea-shore. From the four continents of the world they come: men of all nations and races, civilized and uncivilized, bond and free—Shemitic, Scandinavian, Celtic—from the snows of Lapland, and from beneath the sunny skies of Italy—French and Germans, Greeks and Russians, the Hindu and the Chinaman, Africans and Americans—will gather around the throne of the Lamb on high.* All the distinctions of

---

* "See these pure white clouds that stretch, in ranks like rolling waves, across the canopy of heaven in the still, deep

earth will be forgotten there. Not as a Churchman or Dissenter, not as an Episcopalian or Presbyterian, not as a Baptist or Wesleyan Methodist, will any man enter heaven, but simply as a believer in Christ; and all other characteristics will be swallowed up in *adoring love* to him.

Think of the joyful *meetings* there after the bitter partings of earth! Sense dominates over

noon of a summer day. Row after row they lie in the light, opening their bosoms to the blaze of a noon-day sun: and they are all fair; they are 'without spot, or wrinkle, or any such thing.' Who are these that stand, as it were, around the throne of God, in white clothing, and whence came they? These are they that have come from various places on the surface of the earth and sea. Some have come from the briny ocean, and some from miry land: some from yellow, overflowing rivers, and some from cool, crystal springs: some from stagnant pools in lonely deserts, and some from the slimy bed of the Thames or the Clyde, where living creatures can scarcely breathe upon their banks. All are alike welcome to these heavens, and all in their resurrection state equally pure. May I, spiritually distant and unclean— may I rise, like the snow-white clouds, from earth to heaven, and take my place without challenge among the stainless witnesses who stand round the Redeemer's throne? I may —not because my stains are few; but because the blood of Jesus Christ, God's Son, cleanseth from all sin. I may—not because my sins are small; but because my Saviour is great."—*Arnot's Roots and Fruits*, pp. 36, 37.

faith, and it is natural to us to dwell more on the partings. Let us raise our thoughts to the joyful meetings on the resurrection morning! Think of the joyful *surprises* there. Let me instance Paul and Stephen. Paul was given to the Church in answer to Stephen's dying prayer: but when Stephen fell asleep, Saul held the clothes of his murderers. His heart hard as a rock, he watched till the stones crashed in on the martyr's brain. Stephen would not expect to meet him in glory. Think of these two—the prince of martyrs and the prince of apostles—meeting among the nearest to the everlasting throne! And many a praying mother has died commending her godless son with an agony of tears to God. When she was sleeping quietly in her shroud, these tears were instrumental in her son's conversion. With what rapture will mother and son meet on the plains of heaven!

Those who *never met* here shall meet yonder. "We shall sit down with Abraham, Isaac, and Jacob in the kingdom of God." There we shall see Abel, the first martyr; Enoch, the first prophet, who "walked with God, and was not, for

God took him;" Noah, the preacher of righteousness; Melchizedec, King of Salem and priest of the most high God; Moses, the great lawgiver; Joshua, who led Israel's host into the promised land; Caleb, who followed the Lord fully; David also, and Samuel and the prophets; the glorious company of the apostles; the noble army of martyrs—all "clothed with white robes, and palms in their hands, and crying with a loud voice, Salvation to our God which sitteth upon the throne, and unto the Lamb."

Those who *never agreed* here will meet yonder. The story of the two knights who quarrelled about the shield, the one asserting that it was made of gold, the other that it was not gold but silver—is enacted even among godly men every day. The knights were both right and both wrong; for they looked at opposite sides of the shield, and the one side was gold, the other silver. Looking at different aspects of truth, good men draw different conclusions. Paul and Barnabas quarrelled. Barnabas wished to take Mark along with them on their second missionary tour; Paul was sternly opposed to this. Dr. John Erskine wondered how John Newton of Olney could live in the Church of England; Newton wondered that Dr. Erskine could live in the Church of Scotland. Thus the wisest and best take opposite sides. Some are in favor of an establishment, some against it; some are in favor of infant baptism, some against it; some argue for the use of hymns in divine worship, some hold a strong opposite view; some are in favor of ecclesiastical unions, some are wedded to their own sect. But when we reach the land of light and love—when we see God face to face, and know even as also we are known—there will be no discordant note; but with minds purged from all darkness, and with hearts thrilling with love to the Lamb that was slain, we shall unite forever in the holy melodies of heaven.

2. *Their past history.*

(1.) "They came out of great tribulation." Like Jesus, they bore the cross on their way to the crown. The struggle with sin, the war with Satan, the hidings of a Father's face, the hatred of the world, were so many elements in their tribulation. Each had a tale of suffering to tell. One struggled with a hard and humble lot. One lived in a godless family, and was persecuted by those of his own house. One had to work among swearing comrades. One toiled at a thankless post of duty. One had a bitter cup of bodily affliction to drink, and tossed for years on the sick-bed. One had to sigh and cry over abounding iniquity. Their trials were different, but the trials of all were severe. They all equally felt that we "must through much tribulation enter into the kingdom of God."

But they came *out of* their tribulation. Often was their case desperate enough. Often did they say, "I shall one day perish by the hand of Saul." Often were they like the disciples in the storm, when the waves leaped into the ship and they were in jeopardy; or like Paul and his fellow-voyagers, tossed up and down in Adria, while neither sun nor stars in many days appeared, and all hope that they should be saved was taken away: but Jesus wâs in the ship all the while, though he lay in the hinder part asleep on a pillow; so that, in spite of the swelling seas, they reached the shore in safety, and entered full-sail into the haven of Immanuel's Land.

> "When the shore is won at last,
> Who will count the billows past?"

(2.) "They washed their robes and made them white in the blood of the Lamb." They were once black;—covered with spots of guilt and spots of corruption,—scarlet and crimson spots,—sins in thought, word, and deed,—sins original and actual,—sins against the law and sins against the gospel,—sins more in number than the hairs of their heads. But they washed their robes and made them white. They received Christ for sanctification as well as for justification. His blood made them whiter than snow. Not only did they receive the spotless robe of his righteousness when first they came to the cross, but they came every day anew to the cleansing Fountain to have their defilements washed away. It was *a life-long act*. They washed their robes every day. Every day afresh they said:

> "I lay my sins on Jesus,
>   The spotless Lamb of God;
> He bears them all, and frees us
>   From the accursèd load.
>
> "I bring my guilt to Jesus
>   To wash my crimson stains
> White in his blood most precious,
>   Till not a spot remains."

3. *Their future blessedness.*

By a few inimitable touches it is portrayed—"Therefore are they before the throne of God, and serve him day and night in his temple; and he that sitteth on the throne shall dwell among them. They shall hunger no more, neither thirst any more; neither shall the sun light on them, nor any heat. For the Lamb which is in the midst of the throne shall feed them, and shall lead them unto living fountains of waters: and God shall wipe away all tears from their eyes."

Brother! here is your home, the kingdom prepared for you. Live more in heaven. Set your affection on things above. Learn the new song. Lisp it if you cannot sing it.

One evening lately, after a day of pleasant labor in company with a brother beloved, I drew near my home. It was the house of a friend. The night was dark as we struck across a wide plain. At its farther edge flowed a deep, rapid river, which must be crossed. There was no landmark near to guide, but my friend had promised to put a light in the window, and had bid us cry as we approached the river—the signal to him to send a messenger to convey us across. Even before we cried we saw the friendly light shining clear through the darkness high on the farther shore; it could be seen miles away. As we drew near the brink with wary steps, and heard the murmur of the waters, we saw another light below coming nearer and nearer. Our cries had been heard. The messenger was on his way to meet us. We heard his kind voice, and his strong arm took us soon over. Amid loving welcomes, how soon were our toils forgotten!

Thus, brother, do you often walk in darkness and have no light. With wary and trembling feet you approach the dark river. Your flesh and heart fail as you hear the rushing of its waters. But, oh, *there's a light in the window for you.* Your Elder Brother is waiting. The pearly gate is open. The mansion is ready. The flag of invitation waves from the golden towers. And if you cry as you approach the brink—cry aloud—loving angels will come, and bear you up and away until they set you down among the great multitude before the throne and before the Lamb. There may we arrive!

XV.

TIMES OF REFRESHING.

Acts iv. 31–33.

"And when they had prayed, the place was shaken where they were assembled together; and they were all filled with the Holy Ghost, and they spake the word of God with boldness. And the multitude of them that believed were of one heart and of one soul: neither said any of them that aught of the things which he possessed was his own; but they had all things common. And with great power gave the apostles witness of the resurrection of the Lord Jesus: and great grace was upon them all."

HERE is a photograph of the pentecostal church. Her ascended Lord had sent the promise of the Father. The Spirit had come down like a rushing mighty wind. Three thousand souls were converted in a day. "The Lord added to the church daily such as should be saved." At the fourth verse it is said that "the number of the disciples was about five thousand." A movement was begun whose effects were to reach to the ends of the earth.

There is an idea in some minds that the outpouring of the Spirit at Pentecost was an exceptional thing, not to be repeated and not to be expected, and that the Church in her normal state has no warrant to look for such wonderful manifestations. Now, it is nowhere said in the Bible that we need never expect another Pentecost. On the contrary, if we look at the clusters of promises on this head in the Old and New Testaments—such as: " He shall come down like rain upon the mown grass, as showers that water the earth;" "I will pour water upon him that is thirsty, and floods upon the dry ground;" "I will pour upon the house of David, and upon the inhabitants of Jerusalem, the Spirit of grace and of supplications;" "And when he is come, he will reprove *the world* of sin, and of righteousness, and of judgment"—the plenteous rain of Pentecost is what we should naturally expect. The Spirit is to abide with the Church forever.

He waits to enrich her with the river of God, which is full of water. He will not cease to descend until the last of the redeemed is gathered in. So that, if we prayed with the same expectancy as the hundred and twenty in the upper room; if we received the same baptism of fire, and delivered our great message with the same simple trust in the power of the Holy Ghost, we should see the signs of Pentecost again. The Church of the apostles should be our standard. How far we have fallen! Has not the tide receded so far that we are apt to think there is no hope of such a flood-time of the Spirit again, and that we must adapt ourselves to a state of ebb-tide? Is the Church not in danger of resting satisfied if she moves in her well-known grooves, and plies her scriptural means and organizations, although the life and power of the Spirit be not there? And as the invalid who has long lain on the sick-bed, or been wheeled about in his chair, regards as impossible what is but healthful exercise to a strong man, so if disease has become the normal condition of a church, she will regard the life, and love, and joy of the apostolic Church as preternatural. She will cease to expect times of refreshing. She will preach without expecting the conversion of souls.

To correct this evil, God has visited his Church with times of refreshing in all ages. Within the last few years successive waves of blessing have rolled over our land; and the scenes witnessed in many places might be described in the words at the head of this chapter. It was Pentecost over again. It was like harvest home. You heard the vintage-songs. The change was as great as the change from winter to summer, from the poles to the tropics. "Just as if the temperature of this northern hemisphere were raised suddenly, and a mighty tropical river were to pour its fertilizing inundation over the country." *

God loves his wonderful works to be remembered. With the view of stirring up your pure minds by way of remembrance, we shall speak— first, of the *facts*, and then of the *lessons*.

---

* Robertson's Sermons, iii. 36.

I. *The Facts.*

It was in the year 1858 that God visited America with such a remarkable outpouring of his Spirit, that, according to the most authentic testimonies, nine hundred thousand souls were converted.* The facts were so startling that at first they did not produce any deep or general impression. So little was the subject regarded for some time, that the following year, in his opening address to the General Assembly, Principal Cunningham used these words: "The American revival has not yet excited the attention or produced the practical results in this country which might reasonably have been excited, and the churches here ought to beware of letting this most impressive manifestation pass by unimproved."

In May, 1859, the most surprising accounts began to appear in the public prints of what God was doing in Ulster. It seemed as if the tide of blessing had crossed the Atlantic. Hundreds of earnest men and ministers from this country went across, and, like Barnabas, they

* "The Power of Prayer." By Samuel J. Prime, D.D.

"saw the grace of God and were glad." It is true that public opinion for a time was divided. Some, looking at the striking physical manifestations connected with the work at first, and others, who were rather marvelmongers than reverent observers of God's majestic outgoings, did not scruple to say that it was all a delusion. But the work soon declared itself. And when they saw the whole of Ulster shaking like the valley of dry bones—when they saw churches open every night, and heard in densely crowded assemblies the cry for mercy—when at every meeting they heard from the lips of the awakened words like these, "I have found peace in Jesus; he has taken my burden off; his blood has washed me; he is altogether lovely"—when they heard the voice of praise and prayer from every dwelling, so that, passing along the streets of Coleraine, one said to another, "There's nothing but praying here"—when they saw drunkards becoming sober, swearers God-fearing, publicans and harlots pressing into the kingdom, and every form of vice hiding its head—when they saw popish priests railing at the work as "all madness," or affecting to despise it, like the schoolboy who tries to whistle when he is afraid—when they saw godly ministers of all denominations, Presbyterians, Episcopalians, Wesleyans, Baptists, Independents, rejoicing in God's wonderful works, and recognizing their common brotherhood in Christ in a manner previously unknown—the most sceptical were compelled to bow their heads, and say, "This is the finger of God!" *

The blessed tide flowed across to the shores of Scotland. Ministers came home with a new fire burning in their hearts, and told their people what they had seen. They were like men that dreamed. The rest is well known. The leaven spread. The work extended in some places like fire in a prairie. The summer of 1859 will be forever remembered by many as the time of their espousals to Christ. The Wynd church in Glasgow became the centre of a blessed movement which spread over the city. That church became the parent of at least seven Home Mission congregations; and the record

* "The Year of Grace." By William Gibson, D.D.

of the revival there, in the Rev. D. M‘Coll's remarkable work, "Among the Masses; or, Work in the Wynds," is one of the most thrilling chapters in the religious history of Scotland. The quickening breath blew over the length and breadth of the land, from the Solway to Shetland, and from Cantyre to Lewis. Wonderful how those classes that had been most estranged from the house of God received the largest share of the blessing. Every one knows how much our sailors and fishermen, our mining and manufacturing population, and especially our farm-servants in districts where the bothy system prevails, were neglected in other days. These classes were awakened in largest numbers. The seaports all round our shores, from Eyemouth to Kirkwall, and from Campbeltown to Stornoway, received the pentecostal shower. You might hear the sound of psalms from fishing-boats. Mining and manufacturing towns, despite unsightly chimneys, and forges, and smoke, became as the garden of the Lord. And among the agricultural class, so wide-spread was the blessing, that revivals, which in other circumstances had been very remarkable, in which two or three hundred souls were converted, hardly attracted any notice. At a conference in the Synod of Glasgow and Ayr upon the subject, in 1861, a brother—referring to the awakenings at Biggar, Skirling, Symington, Stonehouse—observed, " So great is the change, that, had it happened twenty years ago, say, at the time of the Kilsyth revival, the attention of the whole country would have been arrested upon it: and had it been *foretold* twenty years ago, men would have said, like the unbelieving lord in Samaria, 'Behold, if the Lord would make windows in heaven, might this thing be?'"

But the movement was not confined to Scotland. From Wales, from various parts of England, especially seaports, from Sweden, from many of our colonial outposts, there came tidings of an "abundant rain." London's mighty heart was stirred. Theatres became houses of prayer—the birthplaces of precious souls. Cotemporaneously with this, the Great Head of the Church raised up a goodly staff of lay agents, to reach those not to be got at by the ordinary agencies. "He took a Brownlow North from the hunting-field, a Blackwood from the Queen's Court, a Weaver from the coalpit, a Carter from his sooty chimneys!"* The regular ministry is never more needed, and never more prized, than in times of revival; but there will always be many *volunteers* to tell the wonderful story of a Saviour's love. The labors of Macdowall Grant, Radcliffe, Duncan Matheson, Hammond, and others, were widely blessed. "May He still spare us these worthy laborers, and add unlimitedly to their number, calling the shopman from the counter, the soldier from the ranks, the lawyer from the bar, the rich man from his club, by his irresistible but gracious message, 'The Lord hath need of thee.'" †

* Milne's "Gatherings," p. 149.

† At a Conference of ministers and elders in St. Enoch's, Glasgow, in April, 1861, where several hundreds were present —the question, How the recognition of lay agents would affect the standing of the ministry, was discussed among other topics. Mr. Arnot said, "If the minister is like a post stuck in the mud, when the tide rises it buries him, and he deserves to be buried; but if he is like a ship freighted with precious cargo, the higher the tide rises, the higher does he rise along with it."

Two things must be remembered: First, Wherever the Holy Spirit is working, *Satan is busy.* Second, In times of awakening, ministers and others cannot be too careful in *discriminating between true and false awakenings,* and in *guarding against excesses and extravagances.* It is impossible to lay too much stress upon these things.

On the other hand, we must beware of looking coldly on a work of God, because it does not tally with our preconceived notions, and is not in accordance with our line of things. Let us rather say, Lord, work *where, when,* and *as* thou wilt!

It cannot be denied that some gave way to prejudice against the recent awakenings, and that even good men stood aloof. Mainly on two grounds, *Dread of excitement* and *Suspicion of sudden conversion.*

1. In regard to *dread of excitement,* it is to be observed that every religious awakening that has been at all widespread, has been attended with great excitement. On the day of Pentecost, the people were "all amazed," and there must have been a strange commotion when three thou-

sand cried out at once, "Men and brethren, what shall we do?"* Paul preached at Troas all night. It must have been an exciting time. Festus thought Paul excited, and "said, with a loud voice, Paul, thou art beside thyself; much learning doth make thee mad. But he said, I am not mad, most noble Festus; but speak forth the words of truth and soberness." In 1742, when a harvest of two thousand souls was reaped in Cambuslang, Kilsyth, and other places in the neighborhood of Glasgow, the vastest audiences Scotland ever saw, shook like trees bending to the blast, under the appeals of Whitefield. By far the most impressive reminiscence of my childhood is, being present one drizzly day, in a Highland gorge, filled with thousands who had flocked near and far to hear that apostle of God, John Macdonald; and as the strong-spoken man poured forth his fervid message in the Gaelic he loved so well, the trumpet-like voice went pealing through the crowd, conquering the patter of the rain on the forest of umbrellas; and long before he was done, the place became a Bochim, a

* "The Tongue of Fire," p. 91.

place of weepers. There was great excitement in St. Leonard's, Perth, and St. Peter's, Dundee, in 1839.* Once more, when minister of

* "I would remark the unusual and long-continuing thirsting for the Word which the people manifested. Night after night, for many weeks, the church was one dense mass of human beings, all the passages being crowded with persons who remained standing for hours together, and seemingly inaccessible to weariness and fatigue. I would remark also the deep, solemn, almost awful attention which they maintained during the whole of the services. I would observe, also, that the awakening extended to many miles around. Persons frequently came in from great distances to attend the meetings, and returned home through the night. I may also remark, that one of the things which was most to be regretted, during the awakening, was the want of a sufficient number of judicious, experienced Christians to take charge of prayer-meetings, which were, therefore, necessarily intrusted to young men. And now, though it was to me a time of much labor and anxiety, I look back with thankfulness that I was privileged to see such a season; and it is my desire and prayer that I may yet see similar days of the right hand of the Most High."—Rev. JOHN MILNE. *Evidence on Revivals*, taken before a Committee of the Presbytery of Aberdeen in 1841, p. 60.

"I have been led to examine, with particular care, the accounts that have been left us of the Lord's marvellous works in the days that are past, both in our own land and in other parts of the world, in order that I might compare these with what has lately taken place in Dundee and in other parts of Scotland. In doing this, I have been fully convinced, that the outpouring of the Holy Spirit at the Kirk of Shotts, and again, a century after, at Cambuslang, etc., in Scotland, and

Stornoway, I often heard old men speak of the *fainting* in the island of Lewis, more than forty years ago, when a great awakening took place, attended by substantially the same physical manifestations recently seen in Ulster and elsewhere. On all these occasions, God was manifestly carrying on his work. Men were in awful earnest. Earth was brought near to heaven. But there was great bodily excitement—groans, sobs, faintings. In some cases, persons were helplessly prostrated, and had to be carried out of the church. Do we approve of excitement? Do we approve of preaching all night as Paul did at Troas? Yes, if *necessary*. And would to

under the ministry of President Edwards in America, was attended by the very same appearances as the work in our day. Indeed, so completely do they seem to agree, both in their nature and in the circumstances that attended them, that I have not heard a single objection brought against the work of God now, which was not urged against it in former times, and that has not been most scripturally and triumphantly removed by Mr. Robe in his narrative, and by President Edwards in his invaluable 'Thoughts on the Revival of Religion in New England.' 'And certainly we must throw by all talk of conversion and Christian experience; and not only so, but we must throw by our Bibles, and give up religion, if this be not in general the work of God.'"—R. M. M'Cheyne. *Memoir and Remains,* p. 501.

God that we had to sit up till three in the morning, like some brethren we saw in Ulster, dealing with those who could not suppress the cry—" What shall we do ?"

Is our dread of excitement a mark of spiritual life? Is it well that crowded prayer-meetings, sermons every night, daily prayer-meetings in town-halls at early hours in the morning, are so rare? Have we not more to fear from worldliness, greed, pride, formality, religious indifferentism, Sabbath-breaking, drunkenness, secret vice, death, than from religious excitement? Many a man has never shed a tear for his sins. If another weeps for his, some call it excitement. Many never attend a prayer-meeting, and if they see others crowding to such meetings they call it excitement. If they hear of a prayer-meeting in a warehouse, or factory, or town-hall; of mill-girls assembling for prayer at the meal-hour, of week evening services, they call it excitement. When Johnson asked a blessing, he sometimes gave a long prayer. The wits of his time called it a mild madness. They would not have called him mad if he had not asked a blessing at all.

People get excited enough about shipping disasters, the stoppage of some great house, the depreciation of stock, the high price of cotton; and they incur no blame. It is only when they are absorbed with thoughts of God and eternity that their excitement is blameworthy. When the Western Bank broke, some went mad, some destroyed themselves, some sank into life-long melancholy. You sympathize with the bankrupt's distress; but if a man feels himself bankrupt in *soul*—in danger of a loss which, in the words of Robert Hall, "it will take eternity to deplore, and eternity to comprehend"—if he passes through the same struggle as Paul, Augustine, Luther, Bunyan, Pascal—you call it excitement. One may stay till morning at the ball or theatre without being accused of keeping late hours; but if he is late at a sermon, he is charged with excitement, keeping late hours, and disturbing his family. It seems strange that it is right to be excited about the passing trifles of a day, and wrong to be excited about things of eternal moment. It seems passing strange that it should be wise for creatures, hastening to the grave and the judgment-seat, to give their whole thought to their shops, and their farms, and their manufactures, while it is but hare-brained excitement to give their whole thought to the salvation of their souls.

But it is said, "Do you not object to the extravagances that attend revivals?" We reply, A stage-coach cannot run without raising dust. I would not drive the coach to raise dust, but I would not stop it because dust is raised. I would drive on, and never mind the dust. "Through human weakness, excitement and even occasional extravagances have attended most great revivals. But of what amount, at this day, are the extravagances which attended the revivals of last century, while the benefits remain? If we are to be used as instruments, errors and weaknesses in abundance may be counted upon. But, oh! let souls be saved; let the dead be quickened; let the filthy be cleansed in the precious blood; let our jails be emptied, our taverns deserted, our streets purified from vice; let the churches and the nations be roused with a mighty awakening, even though human infirmity displayed itself once more."* I have never seen wide-spread concern in a congregation that did not leave precious fruits behind. Satan was busy—some went back and walked no more with Jesus—blossoms of conviction fell thick in the blast—but fruit was gathered to life eternal.

2. In regard to *sudden conversion*, I observe that the quickening of the dead is the work of a moment. The difference between death and life is not one of degree, but of nature. There was *a* moment when Lazarus in his grave heard the voice of the Son of God, and walked forth again a living man. There is *a* moment when the dead soul hears the voice of the Son of God and lives. If the work depended upon man, it would be slow; but he can do it in a twinkling. He breathes upon you, and you live. No doubt the Bible makes frequent use of one important analogy—the growth of seed in the ground—to show that the secrecy and gradualness of the processes of vegetable physiology have their

* W. Arthur.

parallel in the slow and secret ripening of the Spirit's work in the soul; but, lest we should carry this too far, and make a pillow of what is intended to be a prop to the faith and hope of the Christian laborer, it speaks of a nation born in a day, of souls flying as a cloud and as doves to their windows, of laborers going forth to reap the harvest, of three thousand pricked in their hearts, and saying, "Men and brethren, what shall we do?"

It is on the genuineness of conversion that the Scriptures lay stress, not on its slowness or suddenness. Many cases of sudden conversion are recorded there, and will occur to every one. Matthew the publican, James and John, Philip and the woman of Samaria, Zaccheus and the dying thief, the Ethiopian and Saul, Lydia and the jailer, were all suddenly converted. And Saul's conversion was attended with extraordinary physical manifestations. He was *struck down*. He was blind for three days. His own account of the result is, "I was alive without the law once, but when the commandment came, sin revived, and I died." Perhaps you have known a case where a prodigal, long deaf as a stone to a father's counsels and a mother's prayers, after a career of waywardness, was laid on the sick-bed—brought face to face with eternity; and the warnings of other days came back, his heart was touched, his glazed eye caught sight of the cross, and with his faltering breath he committed his soul to Jesus!

The Bible definition of conversion, be it slow or sudden, is "*turning to the Lord,*" and "*cleaving to him with purpose of heart;*" and the test is, "By *their fruits ye shall know them.*" In dealing with awakened persons, the great aim must be to discover whether they have really turned to the Lord, and are bringing forth fruits meet for repentance.

II. *The Lessons.*

1. "The disciples prayed until the place was shaken where they were assembled together." They had power with God, and therefore they had power with men. Prayer is more powerful than preaching. It is in the closet that the

battle is lost or won. Could we but wrestle with the Angel like Jacob; could we but pray for rain like Elijah! It was when Ezekiel prayed, "Come from the four winds, O breath, and breathe upon these slain, that they may live," that the dry bones stood up upon their feet, an exceeding great army. We must go and do likewise. We must pray until the place is shaken. In June, 1861, a great assembly met on the South Inch of Perth—John Milne prayed, and it seemed as if the very ground were shaken at the presence of God. "We will give ourselves continually to prayer."

2. They were all "*filled with the Holy Ghost.*"

They are strong who are filled with him: they are weak who are not. The disciples thought and spoke, lived and labored, in the Spirit. Without him, the best organized church is like a ship without wind, like machinery without steam power, like a cannon primed and ready, but without the spark which would make it strike like the thunderbolt! "*Filled* with the Holy Ghost!" What an attainment! Those who made a near approach to it have left shining paths behind: Charles of Bala, of whom they said that "it was a good sermon to see him,"—Brainerd, who labored like an angel among the North American Indians, and whose diary is one of the most precious uninspired directories for living a heavenly life upon earth,—Nettleton, who preached with such power that thirty thousand were awakened under his ministry. We need many qualifications to fit us for Christ's service: but none half so much as—*being filled with the Holy Ghost*. "Woe is me: for I am undone: for I am a man of unclean lips."

3. "They spake the Word of God with boldness." "They spake boldly in the Lord." (Acts xiv. 3.) They spake as ambassadors for Christ. They delivered the King's message. They spake with his authority.

Not the apostles only. *All* the disciples. "They were all filled with the Holy Ghost, and they spake." A hundred hands are needed on the busy harvest-field. Ministers gather sheaves, others glean and gather ears of corn. "Let him that heareth say, Come." "All that fear God, come, hear, I'll tell what he did for my soul." Remember the blind man whose eyes were opened—how he testified to friends and foes—"One thing I know, that whereas I was blind, now I see." A babe in Christ can say, "Come." In our great towns and mining districts, there are multitudes whom the regular ministry cannot reach. "The Master hath need of you. Although every minister were as a flaming fire in the service of his God, every bishop were a Latimer, every reformer were a Knox, every preacher were a Whitefield, every missionary were a Martyn, the work is greater than ministers can accomplish."* "Would God that all the Lord's people were prophets, and that the Lord would put his Spirit upon them!"†

4. "The multitude of them that believed were of one heart and of one soul." Bound in the golden ties of brotherly love, they were "fair as the moon, clear as the sun, and terrible as an

---

* "Gospel in Ezekiel," p. 14.

† In 1 Tim. iii. 6, where the apostle says, "Not a novice, lest, being lifted up with pride, he fall into the condemnation of the devil"—he is speaking of the "bishop" or pastor. He must not be a novice. But the words do not touch the principle that every disciple should be a missionary.

army with banners." Having found an "enduring substance," they turned their back on the shadows. "None of them said that aught he possessed was his own." "They had all things common." Barnabas sold his land, and shared with Christ's poor.

5. "Great power" attended the Word—"great grace was upon them all." Great power and great grace. Happy Church—fair in the bloom of pentecostal beauty! "The winter is past, the rain is over and gone: the flowers appear on the earth, the time of the singing of birds is come, and the voice of the turtle is heard in our land."

XVI.

"HE THAT WINNETH SOULS IS WISE."

THE LIFE AND LABORS OF THE REV. WM. C. BURNS.[*]

Prov. xi. 30.

"He that winneth souls is wise."

Dan. xii. 3.

"They that be wise shall shine as the brightness of the firmament; and they that turn many to righteousness as the stars for ever and ever."

2 Kings ii. 14.

"Where is the Lord God of Elijah?"

Zech. xi. 2.

"Howl, fir-tree; for the cedar is fallen."

EARLY in July, tidings reached this country that the Rev. William C. Burns died at New-chwang, in the north of China, on the 4th of April last. "Precious in the sight of the Lord is the death

---

[*] "His saltem accumulem donis, et fungar inani Munere."—*Eneid*, vi. 886.

of his saints." This was the death of no ordinary saint. William Burns was a burning and a shining light; and many were willing for a season to rejoice in his light. He was one of the chosen few whom God raised up in our time to revive his work and prepare Scotland for the Disruption. Looking back on the Disruption, with its story of quickened life and heroic sacrifice, we distinguish two bands of men specially raised up to prepare the way for it. One fought the battle in the church courts—Chalmers and Welsh, Cunningham and Dunlop, Candlish and Speirs, Buchanan and Andrew Gray. Another, outside the church courts, preached with pentecostal power that gospel which had fallen out of sight during a dark chapter in the religious history of Scotland; and of all the names in this band—M'Cheyne and James Hamilton, John Macdonald and Alexander Stewart, Gordon and Guthrie, John Milne and the Bonars—none made his influence more widely felt than William Burns. He was the chief instrument in the great Kilsyth revival of 1839, when he was only twenty-four years of age. It was under him that the awakening in St. Peter's, Dundee, began in the autumn of the same year. Mr. M'Cheyne was absent on a mission of inquiry to the Jews, and on his return he found his congregation shaking like the valley of dry bones. "Gifted with a solid and vigorous understanding," we quote the words of a friend who knew him well; "possessed of a voice of vast compass and power,—unsurpassed even by that of Mr. Spurgeon,—and withal, fired with an ardor so intense and an energy so exhaustless, that nothing could damp or resist it, Mr. Burns wielded an influence over the masses whom he addressed which was almost without parallel since the days of Wesley and Whitefield. Crowds flocked to St. Peter's from all the country round, and the strength of the preacher seemed to grow with the incessant demands made upon it." The same blessing accompanied his labors wherever he went—in Glasgow, Perth, Breadalbane, Aberdeen, Brechin, St. Andrews, etc. All over the land there was a sound of a great rain. I reckon it the greatest privilege of my boyhood that I came much under his influence, and reverenced him more than any other living man, and that during my second session at college, when he supplied the pulpit of St. Luke's, Edinburgh, during the temporary absence of the esteemed pastor, Mr. Moody Stuart, I was continually in the way of hearing him and meeting with him. He was wholly weaned from the world. From the day he began his ministry, twenty-nine years ago, he had no home on earth, no family ties, but travelled over the wide world preaching God's blessed evangel. You might think him extreme—many did; but you could not look at him without feeling how truly what a brilliant writer has said of the Baptist applied to him :—" He was homeless upon earth. Well, but beyond—beyond—in the blue eternities above, there was the prophet's home. He had cut himself off from the solaces of life. . . . But he was passing into that country where it matters little whether a man has been clothed in finest linen or in coarsest camel's hair, that still country where the struggle-storm of life is over, and such as John find their rest at last in the home of God. . . . Speech falls from him sharp, rugged, cutting—a word and no more. 'Repent!' 'Wrath to come!' 'The axe is laid at the root of the tree!' 'The fruitless trees will be cast into the fire!' He spoke as men speak when they are in earnest, simply and abruptly, as if the graces of oratory were out of place. And then that life of his! The world could understand it. There was written on it in letters that needed no magnifying-glass to read—'Not of this world.'"* There can be no doubt that his sublime devotion, his Peniel-like wrestlings with God, and his Elijah-like appeals, shot an intenser thrill into the heart of Scotland's Christianity. "He that winneth souls is wise."

There are many definitions of wisdom current in the world. The successful merchant is considered wise. " Men will praise thee when thou doest well to thyself." The man who achieves a name in arms, in the senate, in science, in letters, at the bar, in the church, is thought wise. Or the man who, without aspiring to anything great, does his duty in the various relations of life as a

* "Robertson's Sermons," i. 142.

son, brother, father, master, neighbor, citizen,—whose character is without a stain,—and who is followed to the grave by the regrets of a respectful community,—will be considered wise in no common degree. Solomon says, "He that winneth souls is wise."

What is it to *win souls? How* are they to be won? *Wherein specially lies the wisdom* of him who wins them?

1. What is it to win souls?

The answer is given in the words of Paul's commission—"I send thee to open their eyes, and to turn them from darkness to light, and from the power of Satan unto God; that they may receive forgiveness of sins, and inheritance among them which are sanctified, by faith, that is in me." It is to blow the trumpet and warn the people. It is to save men with fear, pulling them out of the fire. It is to bring a lost sheep back to the fold—to bring a prodigal home from the far country to receive the welcome, the robe, the ring, the kiss. It is to espouse souls to One Husband, and present them as a chaste virgin to Christ.

All this implies that the soul in its natural condition is lost,—lost as a condemned criminal is lost,—lost as the victim of an incurable disease is lost,—lost as a man who has fallen into the sea and sunk is lost. Hear the Bible on the point: "He that believeth not is condemned already." "Ye were by nature the children of wrath even as others." "The whole head is sick, and the whole heart faint; from the sole of the foot even unto the head there is no soundness in it, but wounds, and bruises, and putrefying sores." "At that time ye were without Christ, being alien from the commonwealth of Israel, and strangers from the covenants of promise, having no hope, and without God in the world."

This testimony is conclusive: but other witnesses are at hand. Ask the awakened sinner, and he will tell you that he is lost,—that his life is drawing near to the grave, and his soul to the destroyers. Sinai's thunder is exceeding loud,—the fire burns into the midst of heaven,—and out of the midst of the fire he hears the dreadful words, "Cursed is every one that continueth not in all things that are written in the book of the law to do them." Thus felt Luther when his cell in the convent at Erfurth resounded with his groans, "My sin! my sin!" Thus felt "the pilgrim" as "he read and wept and trembled, and, not being able longer to contain, broke out with a lamentable cry, saying, 'What shall I do?'" Or ask a disciple of Christ—and, with a heart brimming over with gladness, he says, "I was once in a horrible pit, and in the miry clay; but he brought me up, and set my feet upon a rock, and established my goings. Once I sat in darkness, and in the shadow of death, being bound in affliction and iron: I cried unto the Lord in my trouble, and he saved me out of my distresses. Oh that men would praise the Lord for his goodness, and for his wonderful works to the children of men!"

2. *How* are souls to be won?

First, By preaching CHRIST—giving him the highest place, and making all else subservient to him. As the sun among the planets, so is Christ among doctrines. The regal truth among truths—the marrow of theology—the core of the Gospel—is Christ. Christ as the sum of the promises, from the first in Eden to the last in Patmos: the substance of the types: the consummation of the prophecies: the full crown and flower of the Old Testament revelation. We never complain of our minister that he preaches too much of Christ. There can be no tautology in preaching him. The French king said of Bourdaloue, that he "would rather hear the repetitions of Bourdaloue than the novelties of another." So we would rather hear the repetitions of the preacher who never tires of this matchless theme than the novelties of others. Give us Christ always, Christ ever. Christ in the bosom of the Father—Christ in the manger and in the tomb—Christ on the cross and on the throne;—Christ in the loveliness of his person, the grandeur of his work, the efficacy of his blood, the riches of his grace. Christ our righteousness, Christ our peace, Christ our life, Christ our strength, Christ our hope, Christ our eternal salvation. Look at Paul's preaching. "And I, brethren, when I came to you, came not with excellency of speech or of wisdom, declaring unto you the testimony of God: for I determined not to know anything among you, save Jesus Christ, and him crucified." He found endless variety, richness, freshness, in the glorious theme. Christ's names and offices—his words and works—his life and death—his first coming to take away the sins of many, and his second coming without sin unto salvation. This is the theme that wins souls. Christ crucified is the power of God and the wisdom of God: and when he is "lifted up" in the preaching of the Word, he draws all men unto him.

In this age of letters, is there not serious danger of forgetting this; of putting something else—"excellency of speech or of wisdom," learned speculations, science, rhetoric—in the place of Christ? We know what the danger was at the end of last century, when undisguised Socinianism was preached in many pulpits, and the doctrines of ruin by the Fall, redemption by Christ, and regeneration by the Holy Ghost were seldom heard of. We know how it was said of the most admired preacher in the metropolis, whose church was thronged by crowds of elegant admirers, all on the tip-toe of expectation—a preacher whose sermons were read in the splendid mansions of nobility as the most faultless models of pulpit eloquence that had appeared for ages—that "he paid more attention to the rounding of his sentences than to the salvation of souls." Surely a sight to make angels weep! But look at our own day. The most popular sermons, out of all sight and hearing, in our age, are sermons where the doctrine of the Atonement is perverted, where an erroneous theory of inspiration is taught, where the Sabbath is spoken of as a Jewish holyday, where a view of Baptism is given closely resembling the Romish.*

* I yield to no one in my admiration of the exquisite prose poetry of the writers of the English Broad School. One hardly knows whether most to admire the brilliant style, the deep, passionate earnestness, or the high-toned thoughtfulness of these remarkable writings. The late Alexander Smith has said that reading Milton is like eating off gold plate. So it is the rarest intellectual luxury to read these writers again and again. It cannot be denied, however, that when they deal, for example, with the subject of the Atonement, the tendency of much that they have written is to mystify and rationalize it, and to explain away the obvious meaning of many statements of the Bible. So that if a

Second, Souls are to be won by preaching *like* Christ.

He was *full of the Holy Ghost*. The Lord anointed him to preach good tidings unto the meek. Grace was poured into his lips. He spake as never man spake. We must be filled with the Spirit also. The oil poured on him without measure must flow down upon us. "Meditation, supplication, temptation, make a minister," wrote Luther. Most true. But more briefly. *Being filled with the Holy Ghost* makes a minister.

He was *instant in prayer*. The mountains were his oratory. "In the morning, rising up a great while before day, he went out, and departed into a solitary place, and there prayed." Sometimes "he continued all night in prayer to God." It is *this* that wins souls.

He had *compassion* on the multitude. He

---

youth, when thought is tender, becomes "inoculated" with their spirit, he feels positive embarrassment in turning to the fifty-third of Isaiah. In saying this, I cannot refer to the name of Frederick Robertson without great tenderness, a deep sense of obligation, and the reverence due to splendid genius.

saw them fainting, and scattered abroad as sheep having no shepherd. His pitiful eye saw their lost state, and took in their time and their eternity. He saw them occupied with their farms and their merchandise, and refusing the Great Supper. He saw them eating and drinking, buying and selling, planting and building, marrying and giving in marriage, and giving the Great Salvation the go-by. He saw the tempest gathering, the sky covered with lightning-charged clouds. "And when he was come near, he saw the city, and wept over it, saying, If thou hadst known, even thou, at least in this thy day, the things which belong unto thy peace! but now they are hid from thine eyes."

This Christlike compassion is a mighty means of winning souls. Nothing moves the hardest heart like tears. "I tell you even weeping," wrote Paul. Who could resist the argument of Paul in tears? Whitefield was often melted to tears when preaching. "How can I help it," he said, "when you will not weep for yourselves, though your immortal souls are on the verge of destruction, and, for aught you know, you are hearing your last sermon, and may never more have an opportunity to have Christ offered you!"

He was *unwearied* in winning souls. "He went about doing good." "He must needs go through Samaria." He went after the lost sheep *until* he found it. He made it his business to win souls. We find the same unweariedness in Paul. In Jerusalem, Antioch, Athens, Corinth, Philippi, Rome, he had *one* object—to win souls. And he pursued it for thirty years, "In perils of waters, in perils of robbers, in perils by his own countrymen, in perils by the heathen; in weariness and painfulness, in watchings often, in hunger and thirst, in fastings often, in cold and nakedness."

3. The *special* wisdom of the winner of souls consists in two things.

He sets a great *aim before him here*. How poor are all other objects of earthly ambition compared with his! A fortune is the capitalist's aim—"at sixty years of age he attains wealth, a country seat, splendid plate, a noble establishment." The scholar hives up knowledge. The sage pursues, in the silence of midnight, the speculations which the morning began, and tries to extort from Nature her hidden secrets. The hero struggles for a remembrance and a name on the battle-field. The statesman leaves the stamp of his administration upon his country and his age.

But he that wins one soul wins a jewel for Emmanuel's crown—a jewel which will shine like the sun forever. The winning of souls is the object on which God's heart is set; for which Christ lived, and died, and rose; for which the Holy Ghost is given; for which angels leave their "silver bowers," and haste on errands of mercy; for which the gospel is preached; for which the world, with all its complex politics, is kept standing; and when the last soul is won, just as the scaffolding is taken down when the edifice is finished, "the heavens shall pass away with a great noise, and the elements shall melt with fervent heat: the earth also and the works that are therein shall be burnt up."

He receives a *great reward hereafter*. He whom God has used to win one soul will have an increased weight of glory—a star in his crown. Samuel Rutherford used to say to his flock, "My witness is above that your heaven would be two heavens to me, and the salvation of you all as two salvations to me." What a starry crown will encircle his head who has gathered a flock in the wilderness, and fed them, and tended them, and joyed or wept over them, and at last guided them to the greener hills of Paradise, and who can say in the great day of God, "Behold I and the children whom God hath given me!" "They that be wise shall shine as the brightness of the firmament; and they that turn many to righteousness as the stars for ever and ever."

It is not necessary to say how strikingly all this was illustrated in the life of the distinguished missionary who has lately been taken from us. During the early years of his ministry, from 1839 to 1843, he was probably the means of winning more souls than any other man of his time. He did in Scotland what Nettleton did in America. His spiritual children are to be found over the three kingdoms, in the backwoods of America, at many of the mission-stations in China; and many of them are now with him in glory. We need not dwell on the facts of his life. They are well known. In the religious periodicals of all the churches loving hands have drawn portraits of him. By common consent he has been ranked with missionaries of the apostolic type—Eliot, Schwartz, Brainerd, Martyn, Judson, Duff. From every land sweet spices have come in the form of graceful appreciative tributes to embalm his name. Here is one I have received from a distinguished minister in Germany: "I deeply deplore with you the death of that great Christian hero, William Burns. I think, without exaggeration, we shall almost need to go back to St. Paul to discover a nobler type of evangelistic zeal. Such men lay the foundation of Christian empires." Besides, his own Notes of his labors in this country (which, we believe, are very full), and his letters from China, giving an account of his labors there, will, no doubt, be given to the world shortly in the biography which is in course of preparation.

I shall never forget the first time I saw him It was at Lawers, on Sabbath the 16th of August, 1840. The whole country was ringing with the wonderful movement in Kilsyth, Perth, and Dundee with which his name was associated. It was rumored, too, that, a short time before, a person had died in connection with one of his services. A great multitude assembled, not only with the ordinary feelings of curiosity, but with feelings of wonder and solemnity deepening almost into fear. I can remember the misty day, and the eager crowds that flocked from all directions across hill and lake. The service was, of course, in the open air, and when the preacher appeared many actually felt as if it were an angel of God. There was an indescribable awe over the assembly. Mr. Burns' look, voice, tones; the opening psalm, the comments, the prayer, the chapter, the text (it was the parable of the great supper, in Luke xiv.), the lines of thought, even the minutest—the preacher's incandescent earnestness; the stifled sobs of the hearers on this side, the faces lit up with joy on that; the deathlike silence of the crowd as they reluctantly dispersed in the gold-red evening—the whole scene is ineffaceably daguerreotyped on my memory. There was an evening service in the church; the text was Job xxxiii. 24, "Deliver him from going down to the pit: I have found a ransom." It was the birthnight of many for eternity. Last year, when a deputation from the General Assembly visited the Presbytery of Breadalbane in connection with the state of religion, a venerable minister stated that such of the subjects of that gracious work as still survive adorn the doctrine of God our Saviour in all things. Most of the congregations in the district received the divine shower.

Mr. Burns' Life and Labors illustrate the wonderful way in which Christ dispenses his gifts according to the special work he assigns his servants. William Burns was distinctively an evangelist—κῆρυξ—a herald, a man blowing a trumpet. From the beginning of his ministry he was plainly not cut out for the ordinary work of the pastorate. He could not work in the common tramways. Like the Baptist, he came preaching repentance; and with what terrible earnestness he warned the thousands that flocked to hear him to flee from the coming wrath! Like the Baptist, too, he was independent of home ties—lived, as it were, in the wilderness, "making himself grandly solitary for the work of Christ." His very eyes left their light with you after he had gone. His sermon was like the blast of a trumpet. M'Cheyne said of him, "His manner is so impressive that he often makes me tremble." The word on his lips was "quick and powerful, and sharper than a two-edged sword." Let two instances suffice. Preaching from Job xxxiii. 24, "Deliver him from going down to the pit," and addressing the unsaved, he said, "You are going to the pit when you are going to the market; you are going to the pit when you are going to the dance; you are going to the pit when you are going to your work; you are going to the pit when you are going to the church; you are going to the pit when you are going to the Communion Table; you are going to the pit when you are going away to your homes!"

Once on a fine summer Sabbath evening he was preaching to a vast crowd at the approach to a railway station. A tall man, touched with liquor, on the edge of the crowd, began to mock the preacher and disturb the audience. Mr. Burns paused a moment, and turned his eyes on the man. "You are tall and strong," he said, "but not too tall for a coffin, nor too strong for the worms! You are tall and strong, but not too tall for the grave, nor too strong for death! You are tall and strong, but you will soon have to stand forth, one of the crowd, before the great white throne! And how will you face the Judge of the whole earth! Tall and strong as you are, you cannot be hid from God; the rocks and mountains will not cover you. His all-seeing eye is on you now!"* Such words, "like arrows of the mighty," pierced men's hearts, and made the grand old story of the cross thrice welcome.

And yet there was an Isaiah-like grandeur about his expositions of the gospel. When his

---

* See an able biographical sketch of him in the *Sunday at Home* for September, by Rev. T. Alexander, M.A., Chelsea.

lips were touched with the live coal, it was indeed a feast of fat things to hear him. And even when he was straitened, which he often was, owing to the incessant demands upon him, there was always something precious which stuck fast in the memory.

From first to last, his one object was to win souls. His first text was Rom. xii. 1, " I beseech you, by the mercies of God, that ye present your bodies a living sacrifice," etc., and it was the motto of his life. Though a distinguished student, and endowed with extraordinary linguistic gifts, he was content to be " a fool " for Christ. He sacrificed self, comfort, reputation; the love of home, of friends, of books, for him. He lived in a region above the world's praise or censure. He shook himself free of its conventionalities. Though very loving and conversable, he disliked many of our social customs, because they wasted so much time. He did not care for the most perfect ecclesiastical organizations unless real spiritual work was done. He dreaded the ruts into which so many of us fall. To win souls was his aim, and for this he travelled over the three kingdoms—he labored for two or three years in Canada, and "became quite a Canadian," as he once told us—he labored for twenty-one years in China, preaching the gospel everywhere; in the streets and chief places of concourse at home, in the gospel-boat, or under the shade of a tree in China. For this he translated the "Pilgrim's Progress" into Chinese, and acquired several of the Chinese dialects. For this he prayed without ceasing; and his intensity in prayer often recalled the words of Brainerd, "God enabled me so to agonize in prayer that I was quite wet with sweat, though in the shade and the wind cool. My soul was drawn out very much for the world: I grasped for multitudes of souls. I think I had more enlargement for sinners than for the children of God, though I felt as if I could spend my life in cries for both."* He lived in the habitual contemplation of things unseen and eternal.

And what a noble dying testimony! Three months before his death, he wrote his mother—

* "Brainerd's Life," p. 25.

it was his last letter: "Unless it should please God to rebuke the disease, it is quite evident what the end must be; and I write these lines beforehand, to say that I am happy and ready, through the abounding grace of God, either to live or to die. May the God of all consolation comfort you when the tidings of my decease shall reach you; and through the redeeming blood of Jesus, may we meet in joy before the throne of God!" His last words were, "For thine is the kingdom, and the power, and the glory." Not a word of himself: his supreme thought was the kingdom and the glory of Christ!

CARTERS'
FIRESIDE LIBRARY.

First Series. 90 Cents per Volume.

BY A. L. O. E.

1. THE CLAREMONT TALES.
2. THE ADOPTED SON; AND OTHER TALES. Containing "Walter Binning," "Wings and Stings," and "True Heroism."
3. THE YOUNG PILGRIM.
4. THE GIANT KILLER, AND SEQUEL. Containing "The Giant Killer" and the "Roby Family."
5. FLORA; OR, SELF-DECEPTION.
6. THE NEEDLE AND THE RAT. Containing the "Story of a Needle," and the "Rambles of a Rat."
7. EDDIE ELLERSLIE, AND THE MINE. Containing "Old Friends" and the "Mine."
8. PRECEPTS IN PRACTICE.
9. THE CHRISTIAN'S MIRROR.
10. IDOLS IN THE HEART: A TALE.
11. PRIDE AND HIS PRISONERS.
12. THE SHEPHERD OF BETHLEHEM.
13. THE POACHER. Containing "Harry Dangerfield" and "Angus Tarlton."
14. THE CHIEF'S DAUGHTER. Containing "Day-Break in Britain" and "Parliament in the Playroom."
15. THE LOST JEWEL.
16. STORIES ON THE PARABLES. Containing "Black Cliff" and "Broken Chain."
17. NED MANTON. Containing the "Cottage by the Stream" and "My Neighbor's Shoes."
18. WAR AND PEACE. A STORY OF CABUL.
19. THE ROBBERS' CAVE. A STORY OF ITALY.
20. THE CROWN OF SUCCESS.
21. THE REBEL RECLAIMED. A TALE.
22. THE SILVER CASKET. A TALE.
23. CHRISTIAN CONQUESTS. Containing "Bags of Gold" and "Falsely Accused."

CARTERS' FIRESIDE LIBRARY.

First Series. 90 *Cents per Vol.*

24. TRY AGAIN, AND OTHER STORIES. Containing "Esther Parsons" and "Paying Dear."
25. CORTLEY HALL. Containing "Straight Road" and "Jewish History."
26. GOOD FOR EVIL.
27. CHRISTIAN'S PANOPLY. Containing "Ned Franks" and "Red Cross Knight."
28. EXILES IN BABYLON.
29. GILES OLDHAM.
30. A NUTSHELL OF KNOWLEDGE.
31. RESCUED FROM EGYPT.
32. THE TRIUMPH OVER MIDIAN.
33. SUNDAY CHAPLET. A Series of Stories.
34. HOLIDAY CHAPLET. A Series of Stories.
35. CHILDREN'S TREASURY.
36. THE LAKE IN THE WOODS.
37. SHEER OFF. A TALE.
38. JOHN CAREY. A TALE.

ANNA; OR, A DAUGHTER AT HOME.
AUNT EDITH; OR, LOVE TO GOD THE BEST MOTIVE.
MABEL GRANT. A Highland Story. By BALLANTYNE.
LIFE OF CAPTAIN BATE. By the Rev. JOHN BAILLIE
THE BLACK SHIP, AND OTHER ALLEGORIES.
BLIND LILIAS; OR, FELLOWSHIP WITH GOD.
BLIND MAN'S HOLIDAY. A Series of Short Stories.
THE INDIAN TRIBES OF GUIANA. By BRETT.
BROAD SHADOWS ON LIFE'S PATHWAY. A TALE.
BROTHER AND SISTER; OR, THE WAY OF PEACE.
THE BROTHER'S WATCHWORD.
BUNYAN'S PILGRIM'S PROGRESS.
CLARA STANLEY; OR, A SUMMER AMONG THE HILLS.
LITTLE CROWNS, AND HOW TO WIN THEM. By the Rev. JOS. A. COLLIER.
CONSTANCE AND EDITH; OR, INCIDENTS OF HOME.
THE COTTAGE AND ITS VISITOR. By the author of "Ministering Children."
CRIPPLE DAN. By ANDREW WHITGIFT.
DAYBREAK; OR, TRUTH STRUGGLING AND TRIUMPHANT

CARTERS' FIRESIDE LIBRARY.

First Series. 90 *Cents per Vol.*

DAYS AT MUIRHEAD; OR, OLIVE'S HOLIDAYS.
DAYS OF OLD. By the author of "Ruth."
EMILY VERNON; OR, FILIAL PIETY EXEMPLIFIED.
THE CHILDREN OF THE MANSE. By Mrs. DUNCAN.
EDWARD CLIFFORD; OR, THE MEMORIES OF CHILDHOOD.
ELLIE RANDOLPH.
FANNY AIKEN.
FAR OFF. By the Author of "Peep of Day."
FLORENCE EGERTON; OR, SUNSHINE AND SHADOW.
VESPER. By the COUNTESS DE GASPARIN.
ALICE AND ADOLPHUS. By Mrs. GATTY. Containing "Proverbs Illustrated" and "Worlds not Realized."
AUNT JUDY'S TALES. By Mrs. GATTY.
PARABLES FROM NATURE. By Mrs. GATTY. Containing "Motes in the Sunbeam" and "Circle of Blessing."
MAY DUNDAS. By Mrs. GELDART.
GRANDMAMMA'S SUNSHINE, AND OTHER STORIES. By the author of "Kitty's Victory," &c. Containing "Annie Price" and "Lost Spectacles."
THE HAPPY HOME. By JAMES HAMILTON, D.D.
MEMOIR OF LADY COLQUHOUN. By J. HAMILTON.
HASTE TO THE RESCUE.
LIFE OF GENERAL HAVELOCK.
THE INFANT'S PROGRESS. By Mrs. SHERWOOD.
JACK THE CONQUEROR. By C. E. BOWEN.
JAMIE GORDON; OR, THE ORPHAN.
JEANIE MORRISON; OR, THE DISCIPLINE OF LIFE.
JOLLY AND KATY IN THE COUNTRY.
EARNEST CHRISTIAN: A MEMOIR OF MRS. JUKES.
KATE KILBORN. By the author of "Jeanie Morrison"
KATE AND EFFIE; OR, PREVARICATION.
KITTY'S VICTORY, AND OTHER STORIES.
LIFE OF RICHARD KNILL.
THE LIGHTED VALLEY. A Memoir of Miss BOLTON.
LITTLE LYCHETTS. By the author of "John Halifax."
LOUIS AND FRANK. Containing "Three Months under the Snow" and "Frank Harrison."
MABEL'S EXPERIENCE.
THE FAMILY AT HEATHERDALE. By Mrs. MACKAY.

CARTERS' FIRESIDE LIBRARY.

First Series. 90 *Cents per Vol.*

MARGARET WARNER.
MAUD SUMMERS, THE SIGHTLESS.
THE CONVENT. A Tale. By Miss McCrindell.
MIA AND CHARLIE; or, A Week's Holiday.
MINISTERING CHILDREN. A Tale. By Miss Charlesworth. With 18 Illustrations. 2 vols.
SEQUEL TO MINISTERING CHILDREN. 2 vols.
MY SCHOOLBOY DAYS AND YOUTHFUL COMPANIONS. In one vol.
NEAR HOME; or, The Countries of Europe Described. By the author of the "Peep of Day," &c.
THE WORLD OF WATERS. By Mrs. Osborne.
PASSING CLOUDS; or, Love conquering Evil.
THE PET RABBITS.
PETER'S POUND AND PAUL'S PENNY.
TALES OF THE SCOTTISH COVENANTERS. Containing "Helen of the Glen," "The Persecuted Family," and "Ralph Gemmell." By Robert Pollok.
THE RIVAL KINGS. By the author of "Sidney Grey."
ROUND THE FIRE. A Series of Stories.
RUTH AND HER FRIENDS.
SALE OF CRUMMIE. Containing the "Diamond Brooch" and the "Buried Bible."
SIDNEY GREY. A Story for Boys.
OLIVE LEAVES. By Mrs. L. H. Sigourney.
LETTERS TO MY PUPILS. By Mrs. L. H. Sigourney.
WATER DROPS. By Mrs. L. H. Sigourney.
HOLIDAY HOUSE. By Catherine Sinclair.
ROUGHING IT WITH ALICK BAILLIE.
TALES OF ENGLISH HISTORY.
TALES OF SWEDEN AND THE NORSEMEN.
TALES OF TRAVELLERS. By Maria Hack.
CONTRIBUTIONS OF Q. Q. By Jane Taylor.
THE TORN BIBLE.
ABBEOKUTA; or, Sunrise in the Tropics. By Tucker.
THE RAINBOW IN THE NORTH. By Miss Tucker.
THE SOUTHERN CROSS. By Miss Tucker.
WARFARE AND WORK. A Tale.
THE WAY HOME.
THE WEEK.

CARTERS' FIRESIDE LIBRARY.

First Series. 90 Cents per Vol.

WILLIE AND UNICA. Containing "Little Willie" and "Unica."
LIFE OF WILBERFORCE. By Mary A. Collier.
LIGHTS AND SHADOWS OF SCOTTISH LIFE. By Prof. Wilson.
THE WOODCUTTER OF LEBANON, AND THE EXILES OF LUCERNA. By Rev. J. R. Macduff, D.D.

Second Series. 75 Cents per Vol.

AFRICA'S MOUNTAIN VALLEY. By the author of "Ministering Children."
ASHTON COTTAGE. A Tale.
LIFE STUDIES. By the Rev. John Baillie.
BERTIE LEE. 4 cuts.
BROOK FARM; or, American Country Life.
CHARLES ROUSSELL; or, Industry and Honesty.
CHILDREN ON THE PLAINS. By Aunt Friendly.
THE COMMANDMENT WITH PROMISE.
COSMO'S VISIT TO HIS GRANDPARENTS.
THE COTTAGE FIRESIDE; or, The Parish School.
FIRST AND LAST JOURNEY.
FRANK NETHERTON; or, The Talisman.
FRITZ HAROLD. A Story from the German.
THE JEWISH TWINS. By Aunt Friendly.
RASSELAS, PRINCE OF ABYSSINIA. By Dr. Johnson.
THE LAST WEEK OF DAVIS JOHNSON, Jr.
MAGDALA AND BETHANY. By the Rev. S. C. Malan.
MARION'S SUNDAYS.
MICHAEL KEMP, THE HAPPY FARMER'S LAD.
THE MINE; or, Darkness and Light. By A. L. O. E.
NEW COBWEBS TO CATCH FLIES.
NEWTON'S GIANTS, AND HOW TO FIGHT THEM
TALES OF LYING. By Amelia Opie.
THE LAST SHILLING. By the Rev. P. B. Power.
THE THREE CRIPPLES. By the Rev. P. B. Power.
THE TWO BROTHERS. By the Rev. P. B. Power.
A FAGOT OF STORIES. By Rev. P. B. Power.
STAMP ON IT, JOHN. By Rev. P. B. Power.

Second Series. 75 Cents per Vol.

PRAYING AND WORKING; OR, SOME ACCOUNT OF WHAT MEN CAN DO WHEN IN EARNEST. By W. F. STEVENSON.
ANNALS OF THE POOR. By LEGH RICHMOND.
A SEQUEL TO "PEEP OF DAY."
THE BOY'S BOOK. By Mrs. SIGOURNEY.
THE GIRL'S BOOK. By Mrs. SIGOURNEY.
ORIGINAL POEMS. By the TAYLOR FAMILY.
LIFE OF CAPTAIN VICARS. By Miss MARSH.

Third Series. 60 Cents per Vol.

ANNIE PRICE, AND OTHER STORIES. Six Engravings.
THE BAGS OF GOLD. By A. L. O. E.
THE BEAUTIFUL HOME. By the author of "Ministering Children."
THE BLACK CLIFF. By A. L. O. E.
THE BROKEN CHAIN. By A. L. O. E.
THE BURIED BIBLE, AND OTHER STORIES.
THE FARMER'S DAUGHTER. By Mrs. CAMERON.
CHILD'S BUNYAN.
THE CITIES OF REFUGE. By the Rev. J. R. MACDUFF.
DIAMOND BROOCH.
DIARY OF BROTHER BARTHOLOMEW.
DOLLY'S CHRISTMAS CHICKENS.
ESTHER PARSONS, AND OTHER STORIES. By A. L. O. E.
THE FAITHFUL SISTER.
FALSELY ACCUSED. By A. L. O. E.
FANNY THE FLOWER-GIRL. By Miss BUNBURY.
FRANK HARRISON.
THE CIRCLE OF BLESSING. By Mrs. GATTY.
MOTES IN THE SUNBEAM. By Mrs. GATTY.
PROVERBS ILLUSTRATED. By Mrs. GATTY.
WORLDS NOT REALIZED. By Mrs. GATTY.
THE GIANT-KILLER. By A. L. O. E.
THE GREAT JOURNEY. An Allegory. By MACDUFF.
A MORNING BESIDE THE LAKE OF GALILEE. By JAMES HAMILTON, D.D.
THE LAMP AND THE LANTERN; OR, LIGHT FOR THE TENT AND THE TRAVELLER. By JAMES HAMILTON, D.D.

CARTERS' FIRESIDE LIBRARY. 7

Third Series. 60 Cents per Vol.

HAPPY CHARLIE.
HARRY DANGERFIELD. By A. L. O. E.
HOW PAUL'S PENNY BECAME A POUND.
ANNA ROSS. By GRACE KENNEDY.
PROFESSION IS NOT PRINCIPLE. By GRACE KENNEDY.
PHILIP COLVILLE. By GRACE KENNEDY.
LITTLE KATY AND JOLLY JIM.
LITTLE FREDDIE FEEDING HIS SOUL.
THE LITTLE PEAT-CUTTERS. By MARSHALL.
LITTLE WILLIE.
LIVING JEWELS. By A. L. O. E.
THE LOST SPECTACLES, AND OTHER STORIES.
THE GOLD THREAD. By NORMAN MacLEOD, D.D.
MAGGIE AND THE SPARROWS.
MAIA AND CLEON.
MORNING.
MOTHER'S LAST WORDS, AND FATHER'S CARE.
MY NEIGHBOR'S SHOES. By A. L. O. E.
MY SCHOOLBOY DAYS.
MY YOUTHFUL COMPANIONS.
NED FRANKS. By A. L. O. E.
NELL'S MISSION.
OLD FRIENDS WITH NEW FACES. By A. L. O. E.
OLD MARGIE'S FLOWER-STALL.
PARLIAMENT IN THE PLAYROOM. By A. L. O. E.
PAYING DEAR FOR IT. By A. L. O. E.
RAMBLES OF A RAT. By A. L. O. E.
RED-CROSS KNIGHT. By A. L. O. E.
THE ROBY FAMILY. By A. L. O. E.
CHARLIE SEYMOUR. By CATHERINE SINCLAIR.
STORIES ON THE LORD'S PRAYER.
STORIES OF JEWISH HISTORY.
STORIES OF THE OCEAN. By Rev. JOHN SPAULDING.
TEDDY'S DREAM. By EMMA LESLIE.
THREE MONTHS UNDER THE SNOW.
TIBBY THE CHARWOMAN.
DISPLAY. A Tale. By JANE TAYLOR.

CARTERS' FIRESIDE LIBRARY.

Third Series. 60 *Cents per Vol.*

TUPPY; OR, THE AUTOBIOGRAPHY OF A DONKEY.
UNCLE JACK, THE FAULT-KILLER.
WANDERER IN AFRICA. By A. L. O. E.
WHAT ELISE LOVED BEST.
ZAIDA'S NURSERY NOTE-BOOK. By A. L. O. E.

Fourth Series. 45 *Cents per Vol.*

ANGUS TARLTON. By A. L. O. E.
LOSS OF THE BRIG AUSTRALIA BY FIRE.
GLORY, GLORY, GLORY. By SELINA BUNBURY.
THE CHILD'S BOOK OF DIVINITY. By MACDUFF.
THE COLLIER'S TALE.
THE COTTAGE BY THE STREAM. By A. L. O. E.
DAY-BREAK IN BRITAIN. By A. L. O. E.
HOW PETER'S POUND BECAME A PENNY.
DECISION. By GRACE KENNEDY.
JESSIE ALLEN, THE LAME GIRL. By KENNEDY.
LITTLE WALTER OF WYALUSING.
LOST CHILD. By the author of "Mother's Last Words."
MY MOTHER'S CHAIR.
OLD GINGERBREAD AND THE BOYS.
THE PASTOR'S FAMILY.
HELEN OF THE GLEN. By ROBERT POLLOK.
THE PERSECUTED FAMILY. By ROBERT POLLOK.
RALPH GEMMELL. By ROBERT POLLOK.
THE STRAIGHT ROAD. By A. L. O. E.
THE TOLL-GATE. A Story for Children.
TRUST IN GOD; THREE DAYS IN LIFE OF GELLERT.
TRUTH IS ALWAYS BEST; OR, THE NECKLACE.
THE STORY OF A NEEDLE. By A. L. O. E.
THE TWO PATHS. By A. L. O. E.
TRUE HEROISM. By A. L. O. E.
UNICA. By the author of "Uncle Jack, the Fault-Killer."
THE VILLAGE HOME.
WALTER BINNING. By A. L. O. E.
WEE DAVIE. By NORMAN MACLEOD, D.D.
WINGS AND STINGS. By A. L. O. E.

THE NEW BOOKS.

SEPTEMBER, 1869.

The Bessie Books.

I. BESSIE AT THE SEASIDE. 16mo $1.25
II. BESSIE IN THE CITY. 16mo 1.25
III. BESSIE AND HER FRIENDS. 16mo . . . 1.25
IV. BESSIE AMONG THE MOUNTAINS. 16mo. 1.25
V. BESSIE AT SCHOOL. 16mo 1.25
VI. BESSIE ON HER TRAVELS. 16mo 1.25

The Bessie Books in a neat box, $7.50.

"Bessie is a very charming specimen of little girlhood. It is a lovely story of home and nursery life among a family of bright, merry little children."—*Presbyterian.*

Butterfly's Flights.

BY THE AUTHOR OF THE "WIN AND WEAR" SERIES.

Four vols. in a box.

I. BUTTERFLY AT MOUNT MANSFIELD
II. BUTTERFLY AT SARATOGA.
III. BUTTERFLY AT NIAGARA.
IV. BUTTERFLY AT MONTREAL.

TIBBY THE CHARWOMAN, AND OTHER STORIES.
18mo $0.60

A very charming Scotch story.

Dr. Newton's New Book,

BIBLE WONDERS. By the Rev. Richard Newton,
D.D. 6 illustrations. 16mo 1.25

LITTLE EFFIE'S HOME. By the author of "Bertie
Lee," "Donald Fraser," &c. 16mo. 4 fine illustrations 1.25

LITTLE DROPS OF RAIN. By the author of
"Nell's Mission." 16mo. 4 illustrations 1.00

NELL'S MISSION. 18mo 0.60

GRANDFATHER'S NELL. By the author of
"Squire Downing's Heirs." 4 fine illustrations. 16mo 1.25

MARGARET RUSSELL'S SCHOOL. 4 illus. . . 1.25

SQUIRE DOWNING'S HEIRS. 4 illustrations . . 1.25

THE LITTLE PEAT CUTTERS; OR, THE SONG
OF LOVE. By EMMA MARSHALL. 18mo 0.60

TEDDY'S DREAM; OR, A LITTLE SWEEP'S MIS-
SION. By EMMA LESLIE. 18mo 0.60

LITTLE JACK'S FOUR LESSONS. By the author
of "Ellen Montgomery's Bookshelf," &c. 16mo 0.75

HEBREW HEROES. By A. L. O. E. 16mo . . . 1.50

THE GOLDEN FLEECE. By A. L. O. E. 16mo . 1.00

LITTLE FREDDIE FEEDING HIS SOUL. 18mo 0.60

AUNT MILDRED'S LEGACY. By the author of
"Battles Worth Fighting." 16mo 1.25

THE LILY SERIES. By Mrs. SHERWOOD. 6 vols.
in a box $2.50

Containing:—

    FLOWERS OF THE FOREST.   LITTLE WOODMAN.
    LITTLE BEGGARS.   YOUNG FORESTER.
    THE TWO ORPHANS.   JOAN THE TRUSTY.

JACK, THE CONQUEROR. By the author of "Paul's Penny and Peter's Pound." 16 illustrations 0.90

JOHN CAREY; OR, WHAT IS A CHRISTIAN? By A. L. O. E. 6 illustrations 0.90

TALES FROM ALSACE; OR, SCENES AND PORTRAITS FROM LIFE IN THE DAYS OF THE REFORMATION. 16mo   1.50

OUR LIFE IN CHINA. By Mrs. HELEN S. C. NEVIUS. Illustrated. 16mo 1.50

THE AGATE STORIES. By the author of the "Basket of Flowers." 6 vols. in a box. 18 illustrations . . . 2.00

THE PEARL OF PARABLES. By Rev. Dr. HAMILTON. 9 illustrations 1.25

By the Author of the "Win and Wear" Series.

I. ROBERT LINTON: WHAT LIFE TAUGHT HIM. 1.25
II. WEIGHED IN THE BALANCE 1.25
III. GIRDING ON THE ARMOR 1.25
IV. BINDING THE SHEAVES 1.25
V. EDGED TOOLS 1.25

The "Green Mountain Series,"

Containing the last five books in a neat box, $6.00.

DOLLY'S CHRISTMAS CHICKENS 0.60
MAGGIE AND THE SPARROWS 0.60

By the Authors of "The Wide Wide World," and "Dollars and Cents."

The Word Series.

I. WALKS FROM EDEN. 16mo	$1.50
II. THE HOUSE OF ISRAEL. 16mo	1.50
III. THE STAR OUT OF JACOB. 16mo	1.50

A most entertaining and instructive series, adapted alike to old and young.

THE WEAVER BOY WHO BECAME A MISSIONARY. Being the Story of Dr. Livingstone. 16mo	1.25
A SEQUEL TO THE PEEP OF DAY. 18 illustrations	0.75
SUSY'S SACRIFICE. By the author of the "Golden Ladder" series. 4 illustrations. 16mo	1.25
THE GOLDEN LADDER SERIES. Stories illustrative of the Lord's Prayer. 6 vols. in a box	3.60
NELLIE'S STUMBLING BLOCK. By the same author	1.25
THE A. L. O. E. LIBRARY. 37 vols. in a wooden case	33.00
DONALD FRASER. By the author of "Bertie Lee," &c. 4 illustrations. 16mo	1.00

www.ingramcontent.com/pod-product-compliance
Lightning Source LLC
Chambersburg PA
CBHW030305240426
43673CB00040B/1063